LET THE JONESES THINK THEY ARE WINNING

HOW THE TIME VALUE OF MONEY CAN MAKE ANY AVERAGE PERSON A MILLIONAIRE

GUY EDWARDS

© Copyright 2023 - Guy Edwards. All rights reserved.

It is not legal to reproduce, duplicate, or transmit any part of this document in either electronic means or in printed format. Recording of this publication is strictly prohibited and any storage of this document is not allowed unless with written permission from the publisher, except for the use of brief quotations in a book review.

CONTENTS

Introduction   5

1. THE RELIGION OF CONSUMERISM   17
   An Overview of Consumer Culture   18
   The Risks of Chasing the Joneses   27
   Importance of Breaking Free from Consumer Culture   30

2. THE POWER OF TIME   41
   The Time Value of Money   42
   The Magic of Compound Interest   44
   The Impact of Starting Early and Saving Often   46

3. SMALL CHANGES, BIG RESULTS   51
   Creating a Budget   52
   Avoid Impulse Purchases   56
   Money-saving Tips   60
   How Small Changes Lead to Big Results   67

4. STAYING THE COURSE   71
   Overcoming the Urge to Splurge   72
   Staying Motivated   77
   Patience and Discipline   80
   Avoiding Lifestyle Inflation   84

5. MILLION DOLLAR MYTHS   95
   Common Millionaire Myths Debunked   96
   Don't Let These Misconceptions Hold You Back   103

6. WHO WANTS TO BE A MILLIONAIRE?   119
   So You Want to Be a Millionaire   120
   Be Intentional   140

7. INVESTING FOR GROWTH 147
   Overview of Investing 148
   The Different Investment Flavors 154
   Things You Should Consider Before
   Investing 171
   Creating a Diversified Portfolio 174

8. AVERAGE JOES AND JANES WHO BEAT
   THE JONESES AT THEIR OWN GAME 181
   Ronald Read 182
   Grace Groner 183
   Anne Scheiber 184
   Curt Degerman 187
   Moral of the Story 188

   Conclusion 193
   References 197

INTRODUCTION

"*Financial freedom actually means Freedom from the obsession of dollar bills. When the mind learns to distinguish, Between luxury and actual necessity. That's the beginning of financial freedom... We gotta wake up from materialism to be free. Or else, scheme after scheme we'll be ever unfree.*"

— ABHIJIT NASKAR

You've probably heard the phrase "Chasing the Joneses" before. Yet, have you actually thought about the origin of the expression? Well, listen to the story. In 1913, a cartoon strip by the same name was born and ran for an impressive 26 years. The creator, "Pop" Momand, had a knack for poking fun at our human tendency to do things to impress others. And while you'd think that urge would've died down after the strip ended, it seems to have only gotten stronger. These days, it's not just about keeping up with the Joneses; it's about trying to keep up with the Kardashians!

The *Joneses' mentality* refers to the tendency of people to feel pressure to keep up with the standard of living and material possessions of their neighbors, friends, or social peers. It can force you to live by someone's principles rather than your standards.

This line of thinking is often associated with the belief that one must have the latest and greatest material possessions to be perceived as successful or socially accepted. It leads people to overspend, engage in lifestyle inflation, and incur debt to maintain this standard of living. Someone who embraces this lifestyle may need help to be debt-free or achieve their financial objectives.

If you're reading this, you probably feel inadequate or are not measuring up to societal expectations and cultural norms, which often exposes you to insecurity, low self-esteem, and constant anxiety about your financial situation and spending habits. Your thoughts about not meeting societal expectations or norms have taken over your life, and you want a quick fix. You've sought help online (or from friends), but the strategies you get are not yielding positive results, and you are thinking of giving up on yourself.

Hear this—lack of control over my finances almost ruined my journey to financial freedom many years ago. I felt overwhelmed and powerless when managing money and achieving my financial goals. When I set saving plans, I could not reach them because I kept purchasing everything that caught my attention without considering their impacts on my objectives. I usually kept buying stuff I barely needed, piling up clutters in my home.

I faced social pressure and constantly felt the need to keep up with the Joneses, making me spend beyond my means and creating a debt cycle. If there was something my friends or colleagues bought, I felt incomplete until I acquired mine. Although I didn't enjoy it, it was like a race I must run to keep up or outpace others. As I was living other people's lives, my debt kept increasing. I didn't like what was happening, but I couldn't stop it.

I was stressed and anxious. The pressure to maintain my lifestyle and keep up with societal norms caused me high-stress levels and anxiety, affecting my mental and emotional well-being. My money concerns grew so badly that meeting my immediate needs became challenging.

I cultivated several misconceptions about wealth, and those beliefs were holding me back from controlling my finances, leading to a cycle of overspending and financial insecurity. The relationships I built were not helping my situation—they comprised individuals who believed someone must receive an inheritance and engage in risky business to be rich. Others say you must earn substantial income, be in the right location at the appropriate time, lead lavish lives, or attend prestigious Ivy-league schools to accumulate wealth. Since I didn't have any of these attributes, I erroneously believed their fallacies.

If you're feeling this way right now, you are not alone.

If you knew that adapting yourself to societal expectations and cultural norms is the cause of your feelings of inadequacy, would you make adjustments?

Would you try them if someone shares innovative strategies to control your finances, overcome the pressure to chase the Joneses, and conquer financial stress and anxiety?

I understand where you are in your life and what you need. In this book, you will discover the incredible impact that the time value of money can have on your wealth-building journey and how even an average person can become a millionaire by leveraging this principle. You will access high-yielding investment platforms to boost savings and grow your wealth.

You will also learn to prioritize your financial goals over consumer culture. By breaking free from societal pressures and cultural norms, you will gain a newfound sense of economic freedom and stability, allowing you to pursue your goals and enjoy your life.

What are the benefits of reading this book? You will:

- Improve your financial literacy. You will better understand how to manage your money, set clear financial goals, and create a plan to achieve them—this can help you build a successful financial future.
- Increase your motivation. This book will inspire and motivate you to control your finances and work towards your financial goals.
- Debunk myths—this book will dispel common myths about wealth creation and provide a clearer picture of becoming a millionaire so you

don't limit yourself as you strive to create your dream future.
- Build wealth. By following the actionable steps and guidance provided in the book, you can take steps toward building wealth and achieving financial stability.
- Break free from consumer culture. By breaking away from the *Joneses mentality*, you can focus on your financial goals without the pressure of comparing yourself to others.

The process of accumulating the knowledge you are about to discover in this book took many years of studying self-made millionaires' and billionaires' lifestyles. Learning how people control and improve their financial situations can help facilitate your wealth-creating journey. Many wealthy people have frugal habits—for example:

Mark Zuckerberg, *Meta* (formerly *Facebook*) CEO, has an estimated $56.7 billion in personal assets but maintains a simple and low profile. Instead of skipping work or embracing a flamboyant lifestyle, he works 60 hours (or more) weekly in his company's *Palo Alto* office.

His favorite wears are generic shoes, t-shirts, and pants, not the traditional pricey bespoke suits and branded Italian leather designers and clothing choices many celebrities admire. Mark typically dresses in pants and a t-shirt.

Mark Zuckerberg drives a $30,000 *Acura*, not because he couldn't afford luxurious cars. He is simply frugal, even though this is not something many wealthy people live to do.

Warren Buffett, the renowned *Berkshire Hathaway* investor, has an estimated asset of $78.9 billion. Yet, he leads a simple, frugal life.

He still lives in his *Omaha* home—the $31,000 five-bedroom home he purchased in 1958. As a frugal shopper, he didn't change his cellphone until recently, and he does not have a PC (personal computer) in his workspace.

Warren could afford flashy cars, including a fleet of limos, but drives his *Cadillac XTS*—the $45,000 vehicle he bought in 2014. He does not have a personal driver—he drives himself!

Bridge is his choice of recreation; he avoids extravagant events and vacations.

Warren once treated Bill Gates—his billionaire friend— to lunch at McDonald's using coupons.

By continuing to dwell in the same home he purchased in 1958, Warren Buffett has served as a leading example of what it means to live modestly.

Lady Gaga's record label—*The Fame*—stirred the music world in 2008. The New Yorker has since then amassed a fortune of over $275 million and earned several *Grammy* awards.

Spending money is not Gaga's problem—for example, she reportedly spent $60,000 in 2014 to add 27 *koi fish* to her newly purchased $23 million *Malibu* mansion. But the celebrity appreciates a decent bargain. She uses discounts at the supermarket and enjoys negotiating while buying clothing.

Rob Gronkowski is among the most marketable athletes; his fortune is $45 million. Rob is highly cautious about spending. He once revealed that he hadn't touched his NFL earnings and sign-on fees.

Rob has supported himself by accepting sponsorship payments and avoiding expensive cars.

Sarah Michelle Gellar shops for groceries majorly in *Whole Foods Market* but sticks to items on her list each time she visits the mall.

Despite having a net worth of $30 million, she goes with a bag to carry her things since she receives a rebate.

Picture yourself living a life where you have the means to do what you love and be whom you want to be without worrying about money. Imagine having the peace of mind from knowing you have a solid financial foundation and the freedom to make choices based on your values and desires. This could be your future.

My background in Finance and business administration, combined with my personal experience, gives you a well-rounded perspective on the path to financial success.

Building wealth or dumping consumerism is complex for many people, not because they are not motivated to pursue their dreams. Even with the correct information, you might need help to actualize your objectives if someone leads you through the rope (or keeps you accountable). The information you will find in this book contains everything you need to succeed in your aspirations.

Meet me, Guy Edwards—a personal finance expert who enjoys helping people achieve financial freedom. I have the education, expertise, and experience to guide people on their wealth-building journey. My wife and I are trying to epitomize what is possible through hard work, discipline, and intelligent financial planning. Our journey started together in college, where I amassed a considerable amount of debt from student loans and revolving credit. We worked together on a plan that targeted retiring at 45 with $2 million in net worth. Years later, despite adding a child, we are still on pace to retire before 50, with a little over $4 million in net worth.

Despite the common misconception early in our marriage among friends and family that we were broke, we lived frugally, clipping coupons and saving every penny we could. People noticed our success when we started spending a little more in our early 40s. We currently live in a higher-valued house that was just finished. The house was built with a deliberately understated front not to be seen as lavish. Most people close to us have begun to see the fruits of our frugal lifestyle paying off.

We are proof that anyone can achieve financial freedom, and I am passionate about sharing my knowledge and experience to help others do the same. My ultimate goal in writing this book is to inspire you to prioritize your financial goals over consumer culture. I want to show you that by saving early and often, you can live the life you dream of in the future.

If you have problems creating (or sticking to) a budget, breaking free from consumer culture, or investing in your future, you will get the essential support in this book.

Join me, Guy Edwards, as I show how the time value of money can make any average person a millionaire. Your journey to overcome financial hurdles and consumer behavior starts with *The Religion of Consumerism*, Chapter One's focus.

1

THE RELIGION OF CONSUMERISM

"The things you own end up owning you. It's only after you lose everything that you're free to do anything."

— CHUCK PALAHNIUK

Beverages. Household items. Cleaning products. Birthday gifts. Core factors to consider when buying choice items may include pricing, aesthetics, and taste, although many businesses or goods have embedded themselves in culture and society. This chapter explores the dangers of consumer culture and the importance of breaking free from it.

AN OVERVIEW OF CONSUMER CULTURE

Consumer culture (or consumerism) captures the social status, beliefs, and behaviors relating to products and services acquisition or use. Someone's purchasing habits may determine what they do, value, or how society defines them (IGI Global, n.d.).

Consumer societies have two major components—materialism and apparent consumerism (Cook & Grimsley, 2021). Those who practice conspicuous spending acquire things primarily to show others how expensive and abundant their possessions are.

The development of the automobile in the 1950s is an excellent example of consumer culture. After the second world war, many people moved to the suburbs but needed a car to get to work. Owning a car became the ideal solution for the expanding market. This encouraged the development of a car-centric culture that endures till today.

Moving passengers from one location to another required more than a four-wheeled vehicle. It was about aesthetics, elegance, amenities, and power—this became a subculture and triggered the growth of consumer culture.

Understanding consumer culture is vital for many social reasons. For example, it guides or assists marketers in promoting products and companies. Sociologists study consumer culture to comprehend why people behave in specific ways when analyzing their material belongings (Cook & Grimsley, 2021).

A brief history of consumerism

Capitalism maintained its pace throughout the 20th century, turning the average individual into a buyer with an insatiable need. The idea of humans as consumers started taking shape before the first world war but gained widespread acceptance in America in the 1920s (Higgs, 2021).

People have always consumed the essentials—food, shelter, and clothing—but there wasn't much of an economic incentive for high intake before the 20th century. Thrift or frugality applied in situations where survival provisions were not guaranteed.

The late 18th century saw many initiatives in Britain, advertising new styles, promoting envy, and increasing sales. The luxurious clothing, furniture, and ceramics of the time were only available to a relatively small portion of the population. Still, poorer individuals might have gotten kettles, irons, or other functional home items. Those who would have survived on bread and potatoes could acquire different foods in the late 19th century, expanding their diets beyond bare sustenance.

The burgeoning shops and department stores of that era catered to a small segment of the urban middle class in Europe. Still, the extent to which tempting goods were displayed daily in plain view of passersby was significantly increased. The display was a crucial factor in promoting fashion and envious behavior.

Although many people think that a massive consumption explosion erupted throughout the industrialized world after the second world war, historian William Leach found its origin in the U.S. in the 20th century. For example, mail-order sales soared, existing businesses expanded quickly through the 1890s, and enormous multistory department stores emerged in the new millennium (Higgs, 2021).

Consumer culture returned to the industrialized world after the second world war. The introduction of commercial radio in 1921 aided the massive wave of debt-financed spending of the 1920s. Radio provided curious businesses access to the private sanctuaries of the public mind.

The introduction of television increased the potential impact of advertising messages—it used image and symbolism skillfully more than print and radio.

The modern world's emphasis and the constant pursuit of material possessions

Clothes. Shoes. Cars. Electronic gadgets. Americans have twice as many possessions per person as in 1957 and own several modern conveniences that weren't available back then (DeAngelis, 2004).

Think back to stocking stuffers during the holidays in the 1980s. I remember things like travel board games and decks of playing cards. In today's age, it is more like smartphones and Bluetooth headphones. People say those prioritizing possessions are innately selfish, but is this generalization accurate?

Materialistic individuals feel that possessing or purchasing items is essential for achieving meaningful life goals like happiness and success. In their pursuit to get more, these people frequently neglect other crucial objectives. For example, materialistic persons often show less concern for the environment and other people (Awanis, Schlegelmilch, & Cui, 2018).

Someone might prioritize material possessions because of these reasons:

Self-image. We are concerned about how other people perceive us. Many of our worries—the desire for others to regard us as reliable or compassionate—are healthy and reasonable. What counts most is that we are these things in reality.

Some people would develop a materialistic obsession in their pursuit of a favorable self-image. For example, someone might buy a fancy brand vehicle when a generic model would do. For the sake of brand reputation, another person might purchase a $300 waistband when a $50 belt would be fine. These people believe buying pricey items gives them favorable images or a reputation.

Competition (maybe among peers, friends, or family members). The rivalry between us and the individuals we know may influence many of our choices.

Your sibling took their family on three all-inclusive trips last year—so you want similar experiences.

The house next door is undergoing exterior renovations. You're considering how much it'll cost to improve yours.

Your close friend has bought a German sports car. Driving your ten-year-old dependable sedan is now like riding in a kid's toy.

Peer competition can make us prioritize material possessions to feel adequate or superior (Maximize Minimalism, n.d.).

The desire for happiness. Have you had any of these thoughts at some point?

I'll be happy after I earn the big promotion.

People will respect me after purchasing a big home.

I'll feel whole when I find a spouse.

We frequently focus our happiness on uncontrollable factors. The same applies to having a materialistic habit —we blame our lack of joy in life on what we believe is missing, which could be costly vacations, increased income, luxurious cars, or brand-new clothing.

Many people acquire possessions because of their desire for happiness. But does materialism facilitate enjoyment?

How consumer culture influences your spending habits

Consumer behavior describes a customer's interactions with a brand before or after purchasing. It involves how someone behaves or feels after viewing an advertisement (Sharma, 2022).

Clients react to commercials differently but often similarly interact with the brand after watching an advert campaign. The layout, message, and marketing strategy a firm uses in advertisement largely determines this.

Advertisements affect consumers when businesses present their goods and services to them. For example, a company's marketing materials may attract consumers' attention, depending on the chosen subject or format.

Typical consumer-based advertisements target these elements:

Entertainment. Advertising's primary aim is to notify the world about a company, but it may also entertain the audience if well presented. Like movies and tv shows, advertisements (ads) can captivate the audience's attention.

Ads increase the entertainment factor of TV programs. The same is true for online ads, which are so captivating that internet users may mistakenly assume that they are not ads.

Some advertisements even go viral because they make the audience laugh. If people think your ads are entertaining, they will share them.

Brand familiarity. Customers enjoy using a brand when exposed to it frequently through commercials. Generally, a brand's advertising will help a consumer recognize it. New brands can rival more well-known ones by using advertising to assist them in reaching their target consumers (Sharma, 2022).

Meanwhile, established firms frequently run commercials to maintain the relevance of their goods to customers. After viewing an advertisement, a consumer will associate it with a specific brand. The product or service the business offers will attract their curiosity.

Confidence. A firm may use advertising to persuade people to try its product. Someone's belief that the product would solve their difficulties could grow as a result. New products employ advertisements to attract clients for whom they have yet to prove their value.

Ads that feature fresh product lines or variety help rebuild consumer trust in a company. Some advertising incorporates client testimonials to enhance brand trust among consumers—this is a typical marketing strategy for drugs and other medical products. Customers need to be convinced that pharmaceutical companies' products are worthwhile. Thus, there is a need for endorsement-based advertising.

Social perception. The marketing buyers see makes a product a status symbol. Others are likely to follow suit when a well-known person endorses the style.

The associated social imaging influences consumers to desire the products that the celebrity advertises.

Product benefits. New-to-market products or services use their ads to promote the benefits of what they have to offer. For example, adverts from companies with products that address a specific problem highlight how their product may simplify a laborious process.

Advertisements condense the advantages a product will offer its intended market. Sixty-seven percent of consumers who purchase food products are interested in the ingredients used in the food. Parents study products before buying—68% of these parents believe that marketing may educate consumers to receive the maximum value from their purchases (Sharma, 2022).

Motivation to buy. Businesses create adverts to encourage more customers to buy their products. They spend much money on advertising to get potential customers interested in visiting the nearest store and buying what they have to offer.

Ads that show how they solve a customer's problem also encourage potential consumers to try a product. For example, one Statista survey found that 44% of US consumers purchased a product after reading an online advertisement (Sharma, 2022).

Peer pressure and social media can shape spending habits. One recent study on how social media affects Americans' buying patterns found that approximately 90% of millennials compared their lifestyle to their peers. Sixty percent of the respondents claimed that the fancy apparel, vacations, and other things they saw on social media made them feel inadequate. At the same time, 57% confessed they spent the money they intended to keep after social media exposure (Carter, 2018).

THE RISKS OF CHASING THE JONESES

The negative influence of consumerism on financial well-being and long-term objectives is massive. As the desire for products (goods and services) increases, people's needs and demands grow—their purchasing power increases with higher income. But, if they cannot afford these demands, they become frustrated (Shukla, 2022).

- Consumerism may promote over-reliance on labor-saving technologies. If everyone had a car, public transportation would gradually decline.

- Crime rate increases as a desire for pricey gadgets grows, causing more thefts and daytime robberies.
- Personal relationships may suffer as people work hard to increase their income to maintain a particular lifestyle.
- Importing cheaper items from other countries can impede the expansion of regional manufacturing companies.
- Consumerism may also trigger ecological imbalance. Producing more things or erecting more structures might destroy the natural ecosystem, causing global warming and attendant health issues.

People's lives have changed—instead of emphasizing simplicity, lifestyles have become affluent and full of material conveniences. Consumerism is eroding the nation's natural resources. If someone's wishes are not satisfied, it can impair their mental health, leading to depression and other mental conditions.

Striving to maintain a particular lifestyle often results in debt (when buying expensive things you can't afford) and stress. While your body releases the feel-good chemical dopamine when shopping, the feel-good effect fades quickly (Cruze, 2022). Consumerism may promote these situations:

Anxiety. You will increase your financial stress if you continually shop to relieve it.

Emotions. Shopping to curb negative feelings is an invitation to shopping addictions. Since an addict must frequently shop to suppress those feelings, the emotions eventually explode (Cruze, 2022).

Comparison. The root cause of shopping addiction could be a genuine desire to brag or keep up with a particular lifestyle.

A comparison may serve as a driving force for people who wish to boast about their income—they want to outperform everyone else when shopping.

Difficulty maintaining a budget. Shopping addiction or trying to maintain an expensive lifestyle makes sticking to a budget challenging. You have a healthy budget when your income and expenses are balanced. If you cannot moderate your expenditures, your budget will turn negative, putting you in debt.

Difficult financial situations await anyone keeping up with the Joneses—they face the risk of sacrificing their financial stability for the sake of appearance. Each *like* or *buy* you click only grows the advertiser's (influencers, companies, or social media firms) bank accounts. You'll go into debt if your expenses exceed your available funds. Also, your payments or costs will reduce the amount you can save or invest.

IMPORTANCE OF BREAKING FREE FROM CONSUMER CULTURE

Fewer possessions improve our lives in diverse ways, including reduced debt and anxiety.

Much more comes from wanting less—contentment, gratitude, and freedom from the comparison are stunning habits we develop by avoiding the consumerism that permeates our environment.

Letting go of excessive materialism is crucial to living a more straightforward, enjoyable life.

Benefits of reducing and eliminating consumer debt

Increased financial control. Being debt-free gives you more control over your finances, including where or how you spend your money. You have sufficient cash to achieve your saving or investment goals.

Less hassle. After paying off your debt, you will not be worrying about attempting to appease your creditors.

You won't have to track bills, check whether your bank account has enough money to settle deficits, or make timely payments. Also, you will be able to save for emergencies or resolve pressing financial obligations.

Increased productivity. Your productivity may suffer because of debt, and you may need help to focus or be distracted by financial concerns.

You can focus more clearly and pay attention when debt-free—this increases cognitive capacity, aids decision-making and self-control, and improves your professional life (Westpac, 2021).

Enhanced financial stability. Debt-free living enables you to save more money. Job loss, growing family, and other life events are less frightening when you have a robust emergency fund (Positively Frugal, 2022).

Increased savings. Living debt-free makes putting money away simpler. While getting out of debt right away could be challenging, cutting credit card or vehicle loan interest rates helps.

Improved credit score. Paying off debt helps improve someone's credit score, attracting several advantages. For example, you may enjoy reduced insurance premiums and better interest rates with a higher credit score. Also, potential employers who value credit ratings will find you appealing (Westpac, 2021).

Since hitting financial objectives is tricky when in debt, striving to reduce or eliminate your deficits helps.

Benefits of saving for the future

Building up a healthy savings account is an intelligent way of taking control of your money in today's unstable economy.

Nobody wants to experience the anxiety of being one or two paychecks away from financial ruin because of a lack of reserves for unforeseen events.

Saving provides financial leverage for life's unanticipated events (job loss, car breakdown, or other financial situations). Keeping money requires discipline—if you set financial objectives and are determined to achieve them, saving becomes a fun activity (Home Business, 2019).

Help during emergencies. Crises could come as a surprise—when they do, your budget may not cover the funds. The situation may worsen if the emergency involves a sudden sickness or vehicle accident.

Saving money over time can significantly ease the problem.

Eases post-job loss financial constraints. Losing a job is traumatic—it might plunge a family into a difficult financial situation. Savings might provide solace during this period.

Borrowing might be very challenging after losing a livelihood, leaving individuals who needed to be more clever to save nothing to sustain themselves.

Helps finance down payment. Having savings is crucial when going down the path of homeownership.

All banks demand a down payment from a prospective homeowner before approving a loan. The applicant may borrow the money or save it up (Home Business, 2019).

Aids education finance. Higher education tuition fees are relatively expensive, but saving up ensures you have enough funds (without needing to embrace borrowing), helping you advance swiftly in your career. This will benefit individuals who are not eligible for personal or student loans.

Eases retirement plans. Having sufficient money for retirement is one of the long-term advantages of saving. Retirees who depend on a pension hardly have enough to cover their expenses.

Setting aside a small portion of one's income might result in sizable retirement savings, making retirement comfortable.

Benefits of focusing on personal values and goals instead of societal norms

It helps examine money stories. What are your money thoughts—do you enjoy having it or develop a troubled relationship with it?

Consider your attitudes about cash and the financial principles your parents instilled in you.

Let go of negative emotions preventing you from moving forward and replace them with constructive attitudes to help you achieve financial success.

Aids core value discovery. Your core values are the most important things to you, whether they are your family, your job, or helping others.

Core values are parts of who you are and what you do or experience, and they have the most significant positive effect on your life.

Make sure your financial plan takes your values and future aspirations into account.

Facilitates financial contentment. However, there's no restriction on what you can gain; being guided by affordability when shopping is the key to financial freedom (Houston, 2021).

Financial stress and worry are brought on when a person consistently spends more money than they make, jeopardizing their financial future.

Living within your means results in carrying no consumer debt and spending less than you earn. Your finances feel secure because you have excellent control over your spending.

Understanding how emotions influence financial decisions helps keep your finances organized and controlled.

You can determine if your emotions hurt you financially and change your behavior when aware of how they influence your financial decisions.

Positive impacts of breaking free from consumer culture on mental and emotional well-being

Provides options. Living a frugal lifestyle makes your life flexible enough—you can change jobs, go on vacation, combat health issues, or make significant life changes. You have the financial security that comes with having money saved up to live the life you want (Frugal Woods, 2015).

Use modest living to create the life you want.

Enhances inner peace. Our lives become less stressful when adhering to social norms regarding consumption, attractiveness, and traditional success indicators.

Living for oneself and your objectives is empowering—it helps you nullify judgments and not judge other people's choices.

You'll come to understand that everyone has a unique life trajectory, and there is no best path to achieve fulfillment.

Promotes contentment. Living on less, improving your financial situation, and giving up comparisons are frugal living important components (Be the Budget, n.d.).

So, you don't feel guilty about your 10-year-old vehicle when your neighbor buys a brand-new car.

You don't feel sad about your tiny two-bedroom apartment when you visit a property that is bigger and more attractive than yours.

The envy you typically feel seeing someone wealthier than you are virtually eliminated when you accept your financial capacity and learn to live within your means.

You will realize how frequently other individuals spend above their means as you live frugally. Just because someone drives a fancier car doesn't mean they make more money. Sometimes, such persons are heavily indebted.

Breeds creativity. Frugal living calls for financial ingenuity—it requires innovation, whether it's using coupons, comparing prices at stores, using cash-back programs, or making something instead of buying it (Be the Budget, n.d.).

Also, it would be best to be more inventive the more thrifty you decide to be. Exercising this mental muscle or seeing how proficient you grow with practice is astonishing and satisfying.

Potential for increased financial freedom and security by making intelligent spending choices. Every one of us has an individual conception of what success and financial freedom look like. We connect our notions of financial independence to the financial objectives we have set for ourselves.

Accomplishing a milestone or goal represents a step closer to achieving the financial security that takes years to obtain. But some elements of financial independence apply to everyone—these are great stepping stones to attaining financial freedom (even if they aren't your ultimate economic ambitions).

Minimize debt reliance. Financial freedom entails having little to no debt. It involves saving money and making large purchases without having to rely on debt (FSCB, 2021). You can save or invest more of your earnings by avoiding debt.

If a circumstance happens where you need to take on debt, having low debt usage makes it easier to be approved for credit and manage the monthly payments.

Lowering your high consumer interest, revolving debt accounts will help you save time in your budgeting process and save interest expenses charged monthly. On top of the standard monthly fees, over-limit and transaction fees can cripple an already short paycheck.

Terminate the paycheck-to-paycheck lifestyle. You're locked in an endless bill payment cycle when living paycheck to paycheck. But you won't be at the mercy of this never-ending process as your savings develop and you solidify your financial foundation.

You may rest easy knowing that your finances won't be negatively affected even if that paycheck shows up later than expected. Breaking out from the paycheck-to-paycheck lifestyle helps you feel less stressed about money.

Embrace diversified investments.

Contributing money to retirement plans (or other high-interest investment platforms) may determine how financially free you will become.

Spreading your money among distinct possibilities (such as 401(k), Roth and standard IRA, stocks, and real estate) can help you build financial freedom (FSCB, 2021).

If you need ideas, a financial advisor can help you diversify your investments, minimize risks, and increase your ability to generate income.

Years of hard work and careful money management lead to financial freedom. You may work toward your ideal financial future by setting goals and cultivating good spending and saving habits.

Now that you're aware of the risks posed by consumer culture and how it influences your spending habits, it's time to focus on the power of time and how it affects your financial well-being.

Understanding the dangers of consumer culture and its influence on your spending habits, it's time to turn your attention to the power of time and how it affects your financial wellness.

2

THE POWER OF TIME

Would you prefer to receive *$1,000 right now or be promised the same amount in a year?*

Merely looking at it, you might think there is no difference, as you are receiving the same amount either way. However, choosing to receive the money today is the correct choice. Why is that so? This idea is referred to as the time value of money (Cote, 2022). This chapter covers the importance of the time value of money, including the principle of opportunity cost and the benefits of saving and investing early for long-term financial growth.

THE TIME VALUE OF MONEY

Today's earnings are worth more than tomorrow's income because you can use, invest, or grow the money you received today. So, the $1 you gain now is not equivalent to the $1 someone earns in a year.

Making the right choice is more accessible when the time value of money is considered. Companies consider this when comparing projects with different cash flows or assessing the profitability of projects that involve an initial cash outflow and recurring cash inflows (Heyford, 2022).

Investors can use the time value of money to comprehend their assets' long-term worth better. This value also determines an investor's retirement balance. This explains why many investors prefer to get cash now rather than in the future because money integrated today grows over time. For example, savings account deposits generate interest (Fernando, 2022).

The time value of money emphasizes the importance of saving and investing money early in life. Your saved (or invested) cash can accumulate interest (extra money).

Money loses value when not invested—the extra cash that $1,000 could have made over three years if invested would be lost if kept under a mattress for the same period. The money will be worth less than its original value when retrieved because of inflation's impact on prices.

A quick internet search for a TVM (time value of money) online calculator can help when computing the time value of money.

How does inflation and opportunity cost affect the value of money?

Inflation, which is the general increase in prices of commodities over a specific period, causes a gradual decline in the purchasing power of money. If costs grow, a given sum of cash will eventually buy less than it does now (Fernando, 2022).

As a result, money gradually loses its purchasing power and decreases in value. For example, a dollar you earned in 2018 and saved in your piggy bank is less valuable today than it was then.

With free funds or savings, if you invest the money today, it has the potential to grow through interest and other investment returns.

If you wait to invest the same amount of money in the future, you lose the opportunity for that money to grow during the intervening period.

This lost opportunity for growth is the opportunity cost of not investing the money today, making it worth more in the present.

THE MAGIC OF COMPOUND INTEREST

Compound interest is the interest earned on savings—it is computed using the original principal and the interest accrued over time (Fernando, 2022). Money multiplies more quickly, thanks to compounding, and the more times it multiplies, the more compound interest there will be.

Compound interest applies not only to earnings on principal—your interest generates interest as well (Ashford, 2022).

Suppose you have a savings account earning 5% annual interest. If you invested $1,000, your balance in the first year would be $1,050.

Your balance at the end of the second year is $1,102.50 (since you earn 5% on $1,050, year one balance).

Compound interest's magic allows your savings account balance to increase faster.

If you leave the $1,000 (without making additional deposits) in the account for 30 years, your balance will be $4,321.94.

Unlike compound interest, the principal amount is the only factor used when computing simple interest. Earned interest isn't compounded or put back into the original principal when determining simple interest.

Suppose the savings account in the above example operates on simple interest—your $1,000 will earn $50 per year, making $2,500 (principal inclusive) in 30 years.

If you want to amass wealth over a long time, taking advantage of compound interest helps (this concept will be expanded on in Chapter Seven).

Consumerism frequently makes people place more value on acquiring material possessions today, rather than saving and investing for the future.

You risk missing out on the chance to accumulate wealth through compounding over time if your spending priorities are limited to meeting current desires. For example, you spend $500 monthly on dining out, shopping, and entertainment. In that case, that's $6,000 per year—the money could have been invested in a retirement account or a diversified investment portfolio.

THE IMPACT OF STARTING EARLY AND SAVING OFTEN

Time is the secret to profitable investing. Saving early helps you take advantage of the power of compound interest (Ashford, 2022). Don't say or believe you don't earn enough money to save (or that retirement is far off). Over time, even a tiny amount of savings adds up.

This is the perfect moment to begin contributing to a retirement plan, regardless of age or income. The amount in your retirement fund may decrease if you wait even a few months. You can profit from the interest the retirement contribution earns.

The best way to maximize your prospects in life and have a secure retirement is to save early and often. These are fundamental reasons to save while still young.

Boosting savings. Compound growth, similar to compound interest, is something you can gain from investing your money. It allows you to earn interest on interest effectively; you get interest on the principal amount of your initial investment, any additional contributions you make, and the accrued interest over time (Canada Life, n.d.). Your returns will be higher because of the increased balance on which you now have to earn interest.

Enduring unforeseen situations. Market downturns can affect even conservative investors, which is another justification for early savings. That implies that you have time to make up for any market decline.

Yet it can be much more challenging to bounce back if a market change hits you while attempting to save for retirement. To put this into perspective, consider satisfying pressing obligations such as mortgage and vehicle loans while simultaneously saving aside a sizable portion of your salary for retirement (Canada Life, n.d.).

Getting prepared. Being ready is always good since you can't predict when something that will alter your financial perspective will occur.

Unexpected career changes and last-minute trip chances are just a few of life's shocks. You may tackle these little situations by setting money aside to avoid altering your financial goals.

Setting an example. By developing solid money habits early in life, you can teach your kids the importance of saving early and being organized with money.

It's straightforward—the longer you contribute to a retirement account, the longer your money grows.

By starting the contribution early, you have more time to take advantage of compound interest. The extra benefit is that, if you are eligible, you will also receive employer contributions and government tax breaks besides your payments (Canada Life, n.d.).

Early retirement saving allows you to invest your money for a more extended period, giving it more opportunities to grow. Any returns on your investments are also reinvested.

You may have a higher chance of raising your retirement quality of life if you increase your payments in the future. So, don't pass up the opportunity—start saving early to ensure that you are using your money wisely.

Cultivate a saving habit since the amount you save or invest can earn compound interest, allowing you to make more money over time (Paul, 2022).

Assuming an average annual return of 8%, if you start on your 18th birthday and stop on your 65th birthday, saving $100 monthly will grow to $621,000. According to NerdWallet.com, the average net worth of a typical American who is 65 is $1,217,700 (Schwahn, 2022). Even a small savings plan started when someone is 18 can get them more than halfway to their goal of being a millionaire.

As we age and our earning potential increases, saving $100 monthly will seem like a minimal number. However, for an 18-year-old, it could be a large amount of money. You likely will be somewhere in the middle. The next chapter will help you find ways to save that $100 a month and more.

3

SMALL CHANGES, BIG RESULTS

"A budget doesn't limit your freedom; it gives you freedom."

— RACHEL CRUZE

If you're like many Americans, you might discover you are consuming more (than you're saving) and accumulating debt at an alarming rate. Getting into this routine is simple, but changing it requires deliberate planning and discipline. This chapter covers the essentials of budget creation, how to curb impulse purchases, and provides effective money-saving techniques for achieving financial stability.

CREATING A BUDGET

A budget shows how someone intends to use their money or how much they can spend. Establishing a budget helps you plan for all the dollars you have. While a budget doesn't work like magic, it may aid financial independence and a less stressful life.

A budget helps you plan and monitor your income and expenses. You give your money a purpose by learning to create a budget and following it every month (Lake, 2022). You can make smart money decisions and skip the impulse buying with a budget.

Besides promoting financial stability, having a budget simplifies savings and bill payments. Tracking expenses provides a clear image of where your funds are going (Bell, 2022).

A budget motivates you to identify and work toward your long-term objectives. For example, how can someone save enough cash to purchase a car if they wander through life, flinging cash at every enticing, glittering thing that grabs their attention? A budget compels you to plan, save money, and achieve your objectives.

Creating a budget aids a happy retirement since saving money is essential for your future. You can create a comfortable retirement by contributing a part of your monthly paycheck or earnings to your 401(k) or other retirement accounts (Bell, 2022).

If you're keen to pay off your debt quickly, you might need to delay your needs until your debts are paid off. However, you shouldn't have such a tight spending plan that stops your ability to indulge in any leisurely purchases. Every budget requires flexibility because you might have forgotten about an expense or underestimated the size of one (O'Shea & Schwahn, 2022).

You can make a budget following these steps.

List earnings. Your income includes your regular salary and the extra money you earn from side jobs. Recall that you are dealing with net income, which is the amount you receive after taxes and other deductions.

If your income is erratic, review your previous month's earnings and choose the lowest number to represent this month's expected revenue. If your income increases later in the month, adjust your budget.

Write out expenses. Your payments include food, housing, transportation, and utilities. Create a budget category for each expense.

Few of your payments, like rent or mortgage, are fixed expenses. They remain constant each month. Gas and grocery costs may fluctuate, but you may base your estimate on previous spending (Ramsey Solutions, 2023).

- List the remaining costs, prioritizing the fundamentals such as insurance and debt.
- Add miscellaneous expenses and non-essentials like entertainment.
- Use your bank statement to calculate your past and projected expenses.

You'll achieve your financial goals far more quickly if you reduce your non-essential expenditures.

Remove expenses from earnings. Add up your costs and subtract them from your income. You have a zero-based budget if the balance is zero. This budget type does not mean your bank balance is zero. It entails giving every dollar a job, such as spending, giving, saving, or paying off debt (Ramsey Solutions, 2023).

Monitor transactions. Check your financial activities throughout the month by tracking your purchases.

Subtract gasoline payment from the transportation budget. Remove rent from housing costs after making a payment.

Add the cost of the coffee you purchase on the way to work to your personal expenditure.

Make necessary adjustments while tracking your transactions. Adjust the budget to fit your needs—for example, if the electricity payment is more than the expected amount, simply create a budget line for the cost.

If the water bill is lower than expected, transfer the savings to your current financial goal (or a budget item that has gone over).

Tracking helps you avoid overpaying, improve your spending habits, and maintain accountability (Ramsey Solutions, 2023).

Using as little as one account for all these transactions is encouraged. Keeping it simple aids in the ability to notice spending not budgeted or any overages you may have. The more accounts that must be monitored, the easier it is to miss or skip things.

Make a fresh budget monthly. Copy this month's budget and make adjustments for any upcoming changes.

Remember always to revisit and adjust your budget to suit your financial objectives after milestones are met.

AVOID IMPULSE PURCHASES

Let's face it—making impulsive purchases can be entertaining, at least at the time. You wanted to buy diapers but filled your cart with gorgeous throw pillows.

Consumer culture is all about buying, buying, buying! Advertisers and marketers always try to make you believe you need the latest and greatest products to be happy, successful, or part of the popular crowd.

And let's be real, it's difficult to resist the urge to make an impulsive purchase, even if it means sacrificing your long-term financial goals.

Persistent impulse shopping can have a detrimental impact on your life in a variety of ways. It can deplete someone's monthly budget and make meeting normal expenses difficult for them (CreditNinja, 2022). If you're not careful, repetitive, impulsive purchasing habits might drastically hurt your budget.

These are the potential dangers of impulsive purchasing.

Constant financial need. Impulsive shoppers are more likely to run out of money. Your leftover money for monthly costs will be significantly reduced if you often make impulse purchases.

If you indulge in impulsive purchases, you might spend all your money before you get the following paycheck unless you earn from multiple sources.

This is a risky situation—without money, you could face financial ruin after just one emergency.

Buyer's guilt. Negative feelings could follow after making an impulse purchase. When you make an impulsive purchase, your brain releases dopamine, causing you to feel a surge of good feelings (Credit-Ninja, 2022).

- You feel nervous when everything calms down after realizing that the purchase was impulsive and that you didn't need the item.
- Later, when you take a peek at your bank account, you feel the effects of the buyer's regret.

Bulky debt. Using a credit card for personal purposes can increase impulsive purchases since revolving credit allows you to spend the cash you don't have. Impulsive purchases will become riskier and more alluring with credit cards.

Using your credit cards to make impulsive purchases could result in overwhelming debt. You may be subjected to extraordinarily high-interest rates each month to cover the cost of your impulsive purchasing behaviors.

Bad credit. Your credit score can suffer significantly if you carelessly use your consumer credit card to make impulsive purchases.

Your credit usage ratio rises, and your payment history deteriorates when you engage in unrestrained impulse shopping and pile up debts you cannot repay (Credit-Ninja, 2022).

Bad credit can affect your life, including your ability to rent an apartment and the loans you apply for. For example, loan interest rates are usually high for those with bad credit.

You can avoid impulse purchases using these techniques.

Make a budget. A well-defined monthly budget can trim unforeseen expenses. Managing expenses encourages impulse shoppers to stick to their purchasing purpose.

You are less likely to overspend on impulsive items if you know the excess income you have each month.

Have a shopping plan. Determining what to buy and the amount to spend before stepping foot in a store is an effective strategy for avoiding impulse purchases

(Cruze, 2022). If you have a plan, you'll be less inclined to cave into impulse purchasing.

Take someone along. Is there someone—maybe your sibling or friend—that won't hesitate to confront you when making a purchase decision?

Take them along when shopping—tell them what you intend to purchase and ask them to intervene if you deviate from your plan.

Stall purchases. Allow yourself a full 24 hours to consider a purchase. Go away from your smartphone or laptop, leaving the items in your cart.

Develop a mental checklist to determine whether the product is something you need.

After 24 hours, if you still desire it, consider whether it fits into your budget. You can lessen your impulse buying by doing this.

Make shopping difficult. We can shop whenever we want, from the convenience of our own homes—this makes quitting impulsive buying behaviors difficult.

Create some challenges or checkpoints that make you more conscious of what to buy. For example, take shopping apps off your phone and visit the store's website instead. Remove the credit card data saved on your preferred purchasing websites (Srinivasan, 2022).

Use cash. People spend less when paying with cash as opposed to a credit card. For example, one Bankrate.com study found that individuals who pay with credit cards at fast-food establishments spend 50% more than those who pay with cash (Yeager, n.d.).

Create a shopping list. Have you ever gone to a store intending to buy a specific thing but left with more items than you started with? Without a list, you're more prone to make impulsive purchases.

Impulsive buying can harm your wallet and efforts to accumulate wealth. It may also lead to debt accumulation, which could lower your credit score over time and make it more challenging for you to get financing in the future (Caesar, 2019).

Making a list provides you time to consider if you need everything on the list or whether you can wait to buy it later. This helps you stick to your spending plan and safeguards your savings.

MONEY-SAVING TIPS

Do you ever feel like saving money is just too tricky, no matter how hard you try? Maybe despite your best efforts to cut costs, expenses keep rising.

When life gets in the way—a car requiring new tires or a house demanding a new roof—saving money is quickly put on hold.

Nothing goes exactly as planned when saving money.

You won't save a dime if you're waiting for the perfect time—start right now!

The good news is that your budget may get a breath of fresh air by using these simple techniques to save money.

Minimize the grocery budget. Many consumers are surprised by their monthly grocery spending.

A typically frugal four-person American home spends about $961.10 on groceries per month (Ramsey Solutions, 2023).

Getting to those shopping centers to pick a pack of Oreos, a few bags of chips, and exciting treats is incredibly simple.

These modest expenses build up significantly and cause the budget to go over every month.

Discontinue multiple memberships and subscriptions. You probably pay for several subscriptions, including Amazon Prime, gym memberships, and streaming services like Netflix and Hulu.

Cancel any subscriptions you no longer use frequently. Also, when you buy something, turn off auto-renew.

If you cancel it and then realize you can't live without it, consider subscribing once again (if it doesn't undermine your financial objectives).

Buy generic. Giving up on brand names is a simple way to cut costs.

The marketing of name-brand products is typically the only improvement—if you check the box, you see the logo is very elegant.

Generic versions of medicines, everyday foods, and cleaning products are equally effective but less expensive than their name-brand counterparts (Ramsey Solutions, 2023).

Automate savings. Do you know you can save money without even realizing it?

You can configure your bank account to transfer money to a savings or retirement account automatically. Most employers will also let you split your paycheck deposits to automate regular savings account deposits.

Cut cable. Cable subscription costs are skyrocketing—over the last three years, the typical cable TV bill has increased by 52% (Ramsey Solutions, 2023).

The good news is that there are alternative ways to watch television programs. You can save money using cable alternatives such as streaming services and network apps.

But keep in mind—don't register for any streaming services unless you intend to use them. If you register for everything available, you can pay more than just cable!

Purchase a savvy, smart thermostat. Lowering heating bills helps minimize household expenses. By reducing your temp by anywhere from seven to ten degrees while you're at work, you may save your energy expenses up to 10% annually (Ramsey Solutions, 2023).

Disburse excess or unexpected earnings wisely. Use work bonuses, estates, or tax refunds well.

If you have debts, you would be better off using that cash to settle outstanding credit card debt or school loans.

Develop your emergency fund using the additional money you have if you don't have any debt.

Consider saving or investing your extra cash.

Modify tax withholdings. If you consistently receive sizable tax returns, change the amount of tax withheld from your salary—this increases your monthly income and stops you from paying the government more than necessary.

Cut energy expenses. A few changes to your home can help you save money on electricity bills.

Start by making simple changes like utilizing energy-efficient light bulbs, scheduling shorter showers, mending broken pipes, and laundering clothing in cold water.

Although buying new, energy-saving appliances will save electric bill costs, they are not cheap.

Budget for them each month, and you can save enough money for upgrades.

Review insurance rates. People who get their insurance prices checked by experts save about $700 (Ramsey Solutions, 2023). Check up on things to see if there are any opportunities for savings.

Get discounts. Check if there are discounts when purchasing tickets for a movie, museum, or sporting event.

Minimize phone bills. Consider money-saving options if your monthly mobile phone payment and personal budget conflict.

To save money, do without extras like pricier phone insurance, costly data plans, and worthless warranties.

Bargain with (or change) your supplier. The savings may not be immediate but are worth the extra effort and inquiry.

Attempt a spending ban. Avoid buying anything unnecessary for one week or month—it's a contentment challenge (Ramsey Solutions, 2023). While doing this, list the things you're thankful for daily.

Making meals using the food you have will aid the spending freeze.

Avoid shopping in places where you might make impulsive purchases.

Use coupons. Nothing saves more than the traditional 20% coupon when purchasing an item. *Rakuten* and *Ibotta*, like other cash-back apps, can increase your savings (Ramsey Solutions, 2023).

DIY necessities. Rather than spending money on a bench or expensive light fixture, consider doing it yourself.

On your home improvement, you'll save money by evaluating the cost of the materials and conducting a quick Google search. You shouldn't be paying someone to perform a task you can handle. If you consistently miss the mark, you might contact a friend or neighbor for help, so you don't shell out cash for new drywall you can't do yourself.

If you must embark on any type of work—DIY or otherwise—borrow the equipment you require from a neighbor or friend instead of purchasing them.

Attempt a staycation. Tour the local city with your family instead of whisking them away to distant locations. This saves you hundreds (perhaps thousands) of dollars and also allows you to enjoy yourself while taking a fresh look at your neighborhood.

Refinance the mortgage. If you're doing this, it will save you money in the long run. For example, the interest on a 30-year mortgage will cost you a lot of money. You will save thousands of dollars if you refinance to a 15-year fixed-rate mortgage or can lower your interest rate.

Talk to local property experts to determine whether a refinance is helpful in your specific situation.

Say *no*. Today's society values immediate pleasure. Our favorite restaurant's food can arrive at our door in an hour or less.

The show you want to binge is available and waiting for you. Social media ads claim you need this or that right now.

We only need a few clicks to fulfill almost all of our desires!

But saying *no* (to all these) means you can save a ton of money. Building better financial habits requires a significant mental shift. It's also another approach to developing contentment (Ramsey Solutions, 2023).

HOW SMALL CHANGES LEAD TO BIG RESULTS

Focus on making intelligent spending choices when shopping. It helps you save money, pay off your debt, and live your desired lifestyle. Also, healthy spending habits significantly affect your future financial situation.

If you overspend, you might not have enough money if an unexpected situation happens. Create a spending plan to understand your existing financial resources and due expenses.

Reducing monthly household spending ensures you have more money to put toward your future investments or debt repayment.

While saving for the future may seem frightening, make it simple by contributing your extra money in a 401(k) or retirement account monthly. Examining your monthly spending for areas you can make save even a few dollars is a wise step to save money.

Slight changes in spending can have a significant impact on financial goals and long-term financial stability. By reducing expenses and avoiding unnecessary purchases, individuals can free up and channel more money to savings and investing, which can lead to increased economic growth and stability.

The power of compounding interest means that even small, consistent savings can add up to a substantial amount over time.

I (Guy Edwards) and my wife were like many young couples, trying to make ends meet and save for the future. We were determined to achieve financial stability and independence but felt overwhelmed by the high cost of living and interest on debt carried from college. But we refused to give up on our dreams—instead, we focused on finding small ways to save money.

One of our first steps was using coupons for groceries and other household items. We also attempted to avoid impulse purchases—they put that money into savings.

Every week, we made a point of putting money into their savings account, even if it was just a few dollars. We would then make a monthly payment to our highest-interest debt with that savings. Once the first bill was paid in full, you could feel the debt payment snowball gaining speed.

Our persistence paid off when we saved enough money to make a down payment on our first home. Instead of buying a big, expensive house, We decided to live in half of a duplex to save money. This allowed us to put more money into savings and invest in our future.

Over time, we lived frugally and made intelligent financial decisions. We saved money, invested wisely, and watched our net worth grow. After several years we were able to purchase another rental property, all while maintaining our course. Eventually, we could buy our dream home, a spacious and beautiful family home, without having to worry about financial insecurity.

Our story is a testament to the power of slight changes and savings. By making smart financial choices, even in the face of adversity, my wife and I could achieve our financial goals and live happy, fulfilled life. Our story shows that anyone can achieve financial stability and independence with persistence and discipline.

Are you aware that over a quarter of wealthy people routinely use coupons? That's right! It's a surprising statistic, but it just goes to show that even those with high net worth understand the value of saving money and are not above using coupons to do so (Ramsey Solutions, 2022). So, the next time you see a coupon, don't hesitate to use it—you could be following in the footsteps of successful and savvy millionaire coupon clippers!

Budgeting is just one piece of the puzzle when achieving financial freedom and growth. To truly reach your economic potential, you must have the motivation and discipline to stick to your budget, save consistently, and make smart financial decisions over the long term. In the next chapter, we'll explore the importance of staying committed to your financial goals, overcoming obstacles, and staying motivated along the way.

Let's take the average savings of $100 per month from the last chapter and assume you could save an additional $25/per week by budgeting your money. That would give you a combined $200/ month savings plan. Assuming everything else is equal, your total at age 65 now becomes over $1.24M. That is worth a little extra effort today.

4

STAYING THE COURSE

The savings account balance of 57% of Americans, according to a 2017 GoBankingRates report, is below $1,000. (Ramsey Solutions, 2022). Families earning over $500,000 annually may end up saving little or nothing at all.

Lifestyle inflation—saving major threats—can attack the poor, middle, and upper classes. Lifestyle inflation can find you, no matter your monthly income. This chapter offers advice on resisting the urge to overspend and maintaining patience, motivation, and discipline to achieve long-term financial success.

OVERCOMING THE URGE TO SPLURGE

Did your lips twist into a telltale smile while reading this? If they did, we are pals—or maybe collaborators—in our mutual pleasure of retail therapy.

Anyone who has enjoyed the shopping experience would tell you it is more than just getting something you need. Yet, if you tend to dismiss what might be thought of as a straightforward pick-me-up, it is time for some proof.

According to research, shopping can help reduce depressive symptoms and improve mood (Madan, 2017).

Why does depression make us let go of our self-control as if there's no tomorrow?

The fundamental cause is both fascinating and obvious—among all kinds of feelings, sadness creates a sense that someone has no control over their environment (Madan, 2017).

If a public holiday comes on Sunday this year, you could be disappointed that your favorite eatery was closed the night you chose to go on an impromptu date.

You can't do much to change the calendar or get the restaurant to open.

Whatever the reason, one thing is sure: sorrow is frequently accompanied by a sense of helplessness—a sense that one has no control over the circumstances.

Crowded supermarkets might make it challenging to feel in control, which can encourage overspending. Researchers discovered in a field experiment that people in busy stores were more likely to purchase and spend more money than people in uncrowded stores (Madan, 2017).

Differentiating necessities from wants (and prioritizing needs) may help you overcome the urge to splurge.

The idea that you need a new pair of shoes is unreasonable when you have a wardrobe full of shoes. Shopaholics would like to know that a recent study justifies the desire for material possessions by arguing that what we *need* is beyond our control (Torabi, 2011). However, to achieve your financial objectives, learn to resist the urge to overspend.

Needs aid survival, and they include food, healthcare, and safety. *Wants*, which include trendy clothes, coffeehouse sips, and gym memberships, are the nice things you like to have. They are not necessary for survival (Surbhi, 2017).

Someone's wants are limitless, but their needs are limited. While your survival depends on meeting your needs, wants are products of the desire to improve your comfort level. These tips should help you overcome impulse spending.

Skip temptation. Stop going to places that encourage you to overspend. Avoid tempting yourself by window shopping or taking a leisurely trip to the mall. Ignore internet purchasing websites.

Create a shopping list and follow it when visiting tempting stores. Order delivery of the products you need so you won't get sidetracked while browsing the aisles.

Your in-store splurge will be less expensive than whatever you pay in delivery fees (Holik, 2021).

List possessions. Be honest—do you really need that beautiful product?

You must inventory your possessions and determine what you truly have and require before you know how many extra shoes, notebooks, or holiday decorations you have.

You can discover during this process that you don't require the item you had set your heart on in the first place. Also, you might appreciate your possessions more.

Pause. You might give it more thought if you resist making an impulse buy right away.

Specialists advise different waiting times. While some say 20 minutes, others propose waiting a day or a week (Holik, 2021).

Whichever period you select, it must be sufficient to carefully analyze the item(s) you intend to buy.

Plan purchases. Put an item on a wishlist if you've paused and still want to purchase it. You might ask for the item as a gift on your birthday or a special occasion like Christmas by sharing it with your loved ones.

Plan for making the purchase yourself if you intend to. Set aside a specified amount of money monthly or with each paycheck and add it to your budget.

Saving money over time enables you to make your purchase without fear.

Make an estimate. Determine the time to purchase a specific product by comparing its cost to your hourly wage.

Does the thing merit a full day's labor? You alone know. Nonetheless, doing the math will help you understand the value of your purchase.

Budget for fun activities. There will be instances when you want to purchase something outside your spending limit. Who says you can't spend money on enjoyable things?

You can indulge guilt-free and maintain control over your spending if you plan and account for periodic splurges.

Find perks besides shopping. Do you purchase a treat when feeling depressed (or after completing an extensive project)?

Individuals frequently use purchases to gratify or boost their egos. Instead, look for enjoyable and satisfying treats that cost little money. For example, you could borrow an excellent book or film from the library or go hiking with a friend.

Trade or rent. Use the tools at your disposal to reduce spending.

Exchange a similar item in a transaction with a pal. Ask if you could occasionally borrow something you need from a friend or colleague. You might also consider renting.

All these strategies need little or no financial payment compared to an outright purchase.

STAYING MOTIVATED

Motivation and setting clear goals are closely related in the context of personal finance. When individuals have clear and specific financial goals, they feel motivated to take action toward achieving them. This motivation can help individuals stay focused and disciplined in their financial journey, even when faced with obstacles or temptations to deviate from their budget or spending plan.

Suppose you have a clear goal of saving to purchase a house or car in the next five years. You may feel more motivated to save money, reduce expenses, and make smart financial decisions to achieve that goal. This sense of purpose and direction can help you stay focused and avoid impulse purchases or unwise financial decisions that could jeopardize your progress.

Still, you need clear financial goals to feel more motivated to take control of your finances and make positive changes. This lack of motivation can lead to impulsive spending, poor financial planning, and a failure to make progress toward financial stability and growth.

Part of staying motivated is celebrating minor victories and tracking your progress. People feel happier and are more motivated when they celebrate modest accomplishments. The more someone experiences progress, the more they stick to their goals and are successful (UFCU, 2020).

Be inspired by your minor accomplishments. Please make a note of your progress, show it to a close friend, check off your monthly spending plan in bold green letters, and stick it on the wall or refrigerator.

Do whatever makes you feel successful, and then use that feeling as fuel to get started on your next small objective.

Transformation takes time to manifest. Your success may depend on your capacity to recognize the immediate advantages of your long-term objectives, even when paying off debt, starting a business, or restoring your finances. And when you acknowledge those little successes, you encourage yourself to move forward (UFCU, 2020).

Minor victories are a sign of progress. A string of victories exposes a pattern of productive actions that boosts trust and quells criticism of what is seen as inaction or a lack of progress.

Results come from minor victories. Since they increase commitment to an action plan, small wins achieve outcomes. People are drawn to small successes, and stakeholders are motivated to keep up their engagement.

Little victories show observable development and a winning mentality. Celebrating triumphs strengthens adherence to long-term objectives since it creates a culture of success (Shelton, n.d.).

Being surrounded by supportive friends can be motivating. The people in your life have a profound effect on you. They can positively or negatively affect your feelings, ideas, and actions. Select carefully (Machina, n.d.).

Spending time with the wrong people is a waste of time —they will drag you down, and you'll struggle to realize your full potential. Conversely, associating with prosperous people may support your development and progress toward your objectives.

Having a support system can help you stay motivated and on track, especially during challenging times. For example, if you have friends or family members who share your financial goals and values, they can provide encouragement and advice when you need it most. They can also hold you accountable for your spending and savings decisions, helping you stay focused and disciplined on your financial journey.

Being part of a supportive community can help you stay motivated and inspired. Seeing others making positive changes and achieving their financial goals can serve as a reminder of what is possible and provide the motivation you need to keep going.

PATIENCE AND DISCIPLINE

Each person's financial journey is unique. It would be best if you had the patience to save money, get rid of debt, or put money into retirement investments. Learning to control your emotions is crucial when striving to be financially free. You will progress quickly if you have patience and are responsible and appreciative.

These three factors highlight the importance of patience and discipline when building prosperity.

Market cycles. Investment markets typically move in cycles. A stretch of below-average returns follows above-average returns.

You will need to hold on to an asset longer if you invest at a period of flat growth to produce near-long-term average returns. For example, you must own property for at least ten years to receive the long-term average return pegged at 7 or 8% yearly (Wemyss, 2022).

However, you must own the house for 15 to 20 years if you invest in a flat period.

Returns compound. Capital growth takes time to compound.

Suppose you make a one-time $5,000 contribution in a 7% annual interest rate investment platform. Your balance after five years is $7,013. If the money stays there for ten years, you will get $9,836.

Money compounds with time—this justifies early saving and investing.

Transaction costs. Because of transaction expenses and taxes, altering your investments or approach merely out of impatience may hurt your wealth-building efforts. Yet, this does not mean that you should never make adjustments.

It would be best to make the adjustments as quickly as possible after making a strategic error or poor investment. Refrain from making a change just because you're impatient or the market has yet to produce returns within the expected time.

Long-term outcomes depend on following the fundamentals. Fears and uncertainty affect many investors because it is in our nature to anticipate danger and steer clear of it.

We can be affected by bad news—perhaps this is why negative information is so appealing to media outlets. But we must constantly remind ourselves that the essentials remain constant. Also, bad things happen and disappear, but fundamental truths never change (Wemyss, 2022).

So, if you support your initial investment choice with solid fundamentals, you only need to change it if there is convincing proof that the fundamentals have changed.

Staying disciplined, patient, and consistent in saving and investing can improve your financial journey. You increase your chances of reaching your financial objectives by practicing self-control and overcoming impulse buying. For example, you could stop drinking coffee every day to save for your coming vacation. You could also make monthly contributions to your 401(k) or Roth IRA account to create a comfortable future.

Benefits of avoiding instant gratification and focusing on long-term financial stability

Delayed gratification is the capacity to withstand the lure of an immediate benefit in favor of a later payoff (Carlson, 2022). Applying this to your financial objectives entails choosing to invest or save your money rather than blowing it on frivolous items.

Delaying gratification has several advantages, including speeding up the triumph of your financial objectives and increasing the amount of cash available for unforeseen costs.

Being able to postpone gratification enables you to concentrate on your objectives. When short-term temptations are not continuously luring you away, you have more time and energy to devote to attaining your long-term goals. Another advantage of delayed pleasure is that it helps you develop self-discipline.

Learn to manage your urges if you want to practice delayed gratification. Several aspects of your life may benefit from having this talent. For example, people who delay gratification, according to studies, live happy, content lives (Carlson, 2022). So, if you want to improve your way of life, being able to postpone gratification is a vital success indicator.

Self-control is required to make wise financial judgments. Repressing the desire to splurge cash on material things might be challenging. Delaying gratification increases a person's likelihood of reaching their long-term financial objectives.

You'll have sufficient cash to invest and save when able to keep to a budget and control your impulse to indulge. You can also avoid debt by postponing gratification. Avoiding impulsive expenses decreases the likelihood of using credit to survive.

Consider your long-term objectives the next time you have a spending urge.

AVOIDING LIFESTYLE INFLATION

You started your first full-time work in an entry-level position, and your starting pay was $35,000 yearly. You prepared coffee at home daily but occasionally treated yourself to a latte from a coffee shop.

Your compensation increased to $50,000 after six months, thanks to a well-earned promotion and raise. The once-weekly visit to the coffee store is now a daily ritual. You no longer shop at second-hand stores; instead, you visit high-end department marts.

Lifestyle inflation describes an increase in expense when income rises. Every time a person receives a raise, lifestyle inflation soars, making it difficult for people to pay off debt, prepare for retirement, or accomplish other major financial objectives (Kenton, 2020). Individuals living paycheck to paycheck only have money to cover their monthly expenses; they are trapped in a cycle of lifestyle inflation.

Changing from being a student to becoming a full-time worker is one situation where lifestyle inflation often occurs. Even while you can survive on a tight budget as a student, you may turn luxuries into necessities once you start getting paid, leading to higher spending.

It suddenly doesn't seem appealing to split a two-bedroom flat with three other people to save on rent and utilities as someone makes money. A person who suffers lifestyle inflation may decide to rent a one-bedroom apartment to live alone.

Today's society makes it simple to constantly improve your lifestyle and get caught up in the newest fads without recognizing them. This phenomenon can be a trap that keeps you from achieving your financial objectives. You put short-term pleasure ahead of long-term financial stability every time you raise your expenditure.

If you want to accumulate wealth and enjoy financial freedom, you must moderate your standard of living and prioritize your financial future over the transient pleasures of materialism.

Dangers of lifestyle inflation and its impacts on financial stability.

Inflated living cost. If you're not mindful of your spending limits, lifestyle inflation might make your payments out of control (Thrivent, 2022).

Suppose your job pays you $50,000 a year. Your annual salary increases to $70,000 after earning a raise. You buy a new car because your salary has increased—after all, you've been driving that old beater for eight years.

Suddenly, as your confidence grows, you go on a pricey road trip with your pals in the new car.

Even with a better income, you can have trouble making ends meet if you aren't monitoring your finances carefully and making the adjustments to your budget.

Saving money or making debt payments can be difficult when income increases but, expenditures increase as fast or faster—this may trigger financial difficulties in the future.

Fewer savings. Saving money gets difficult when spending rises in tandem with income—you spend additional funds instead of putting them into your savings account.

You might not be ready for emergencies (since you have no savings). Sickness or an unexpected layoff could put you at risk of failing to cover essential living costs (My Money Yard, 2022).

Saving for major life events like weddings and holidays becomes tough. You would likely lose out on compound interest, another significant disadvantage of lifestyle inflation.

Money waste. Without exercising caution, an increase in spending will cause money loss. For example, you might be paying for subscriptions you don't use or financing purchases with higher interest rates than necessary.

You might say you don't need a budget or practice financial restraint because of your comfortable living standard and income—these irrational costs will go unnoticed when this is the case.

Debt risk. A limited ability to save may increase the risk of going into debt. For example, using a credit card for additional purchases becomes unavoidable when expenses tally more than income.

You might need to get a loan to cover emergencies.

Unless your credit card charges 0% interest, these commitments attract charges.

Living within your means and focusing on financial security over material possessions can give you more profound joy. Maybe you could afford a larger home, opulent travel, or expensive furniture—you can achieve inner happiness and satisfaction by preventing your spending from surpassing your income (My Money Yard, 2022).

These tips will help you avoid the trap of constantly wanting more and spending more.

Halt and rethink. Examine your life. Do you have the resources—time, money, and energy—to prioritize what matters?

Has having things prevented you from focusing on your financial objectives?

Calm down to objectively assess your income, mortgage, spending patterns, and daily activities.

Are you content (or is there something you want to do differently)?

Quit imitating others. Don't pursue a particular way of life just because your friends, classmates, and neighbors are. You can't live the same life as everyone else.

You are mistaken if you believe that adhering to the most recent trends in society will make you happier (Becker, n.d.).

Know your flaws. Learn your triggers. Are there any stores where you feel compelled to make needless purchases?

Do certain goods, habits, or pricing trends make you react instantly?

Some emotions—like sadness, loneliness, and grief—cause people to consume things mindlessly (Becker, n.d.).

Examine your driving forces. Marketers appeal subtly to consumers' motivations to manipulate them. Product facts are no longer the foundation of advertisements. Suppliers make promises of excitement, respect, happiness, and fulfillment when advertising their products.

What underlying motives influence your purchases? What drives—greed or envy—do you need to eliminate?

Strive for utility and life-saving contributions when making purchases. Living means consuming—we work, earn money, make purchases, and consume. But, apart from being consumers, we are contributors. We should make our existence on this planet valuable to the surrounding people.

Buy what you require to fulfill your particular function in this life; everything else is a diversion. Don't purchase anything just because you can.

Track each purchase's extra costs. We solely consider the sticker price when making purchases. Since this is only sometimes the total price, we end up paying more for the things we buy.

Cleaning, arranging, or mending the items we purchase requires attention, effort, and time, causing us stress and anxiety.

Your trade for anything determines its price.

Explore your boundaries. Try the challenge of not shopping—don't spend on anything for one month, visit no stores for 60 days, or avoid clothing marts for 120 days.

While you'll stop the cycle of shopping in the short term, you'll create a stronger foundation for success in the long run (Becker, n.d.).

Make donations. Giving can warm your heart, helping you improve the world.

Expand on your pleasurable activities. You're not happy because of your possessions because the satisfaction we find in materialism is short (Becker, n.d.).

Identify and do more of what brings you joy. Some individuals find happiness in their faith, family, friends, or helping others.

Make intentionality (the opposite of consumerism) your primary goal.

My good friend, Richard, received a big promotion at work, complete with a substantial salary increase. At first, he was thrilled about the extra income and the recognition of his hard work. But as time passed, I noticed that his financial situation wasn't improving. Despite the extra money, Richard still lived paycheck to paycheck and struggled with debt.

One day, I asked Richard what was going on and learned that he was trying to keep up with the higher-level executives at work and the business' clients and partners. He felt he needed to project a particular image of success and wealth to fit in with these influential people. But it wasn't just about fitting in. Richard had also developed an "I deserve this" mentality because of how hard he was working.

He thought his hard work deserved to be rewarded with fancy dinners, expensive vacations, and luxury items. So, he started spending more money to keep up with the Joneses and to reward himself. So, Richard's financial situation wasn't improving. He was still living paycheck to paycheck and struggling with debt, even though he was making more money.

He had fallen into the trap of mindless consumption, thinking that keeping up with the higher-ups at work and rewarding himself for his hard work would bring him success, but it only created more financial problems.

Richard's story is a cautionary tale about the dangers of lifestyle inflation, the pressure to fit in with our peers, and the "I deserve this" mentality. Spending more money when we feel like we need to project a certain image or reward ourselves for our hard work is relatively straightforward. Still, it's important to remember that more money doesn't always equal more financial stability. Throughout our discussions, we've stressed the need to resist the urge to splurge and maintain our attention on our long-term financial objectives. It's not always easy, but with patience, motivation, and discipline, you can overcome the challenges, reach financial stability and growth—and even become a millionaire!

Earlier in this chapter, we talked about getting a promotion and a coffee stop becoming daily. Imagine that you took that $7 per day coffee expense and started putting that into your employer's 401k plan. $7/day would be, on average, $140 per month. From age 20 to 65, that would end up being an additional

$1.47M in addition to the $1.2M you are currently on pace to save in our previous examples, taking your retirement total to $2.6M.

But there are also many myths about becoming a millionaire. People often think you need to be born into wealth, have a high-paying job, or win the lottery to become a millionaire. But the truth is, anyone can become a millionaire with the right mindset and approach to their finances. That's why, in the next chapter, we're going to bust some of the biggest myths about millionaires and show you how you can achieve financial success, regardless of your starting point.

5

MILLION DOLLAR MYTHS

Many false beliefs and misunderstandings surround millionaires, which often prevent people from pursuing their financial goals and success. These myths can lead people to believe that becoming a millionaire is impossible or only achievable through means outside of their control. However, anyone can become a millionaire with the right mindset, approach to their finances, and determination to reach their financial goals.

So, let's tackle these myths one by one and empower you to take control of your financial destiny. This chapter busts prevalent misconceptions about millionaires, highlights the drawbacks of holding onto these myths and inspires you to take control of your finances.

COMMON MILLIONAIRE MYTHS DEBUNKED

Many people believe they will never become millionaires, even though things work well for them. Some feel it is an entirely unreachable dream. What's preventing some people from reaching financial success is their wrong mindset.

Ten thousand people took part in the largest poll of millionaires ever done by Ramsey Solutions (Ramsey Solutions, 2022). Findings showed that:

- Eighty percent of self-made millionaires invested in 401(k) and other retirement accounts.
- The top five professions for millionaires are engineering, accounting, teaching, management, and law.
- Seventy-nine percent of millionaires have no inheritance from parents or other relatives at all.

Some Americans feel they lack what it takes to create wealth even though America is considered a land of opportunities (Ramsey Solutions, 2022). They have bought into the lie that having a high income or coming from a wealthy family makes someone a millionaire. Ramsey Solutions' study of millionaires has debunked the misconceptions about how rich people gain their wealth.

So, how did these millionaires accumulate their fortune? Most of them achieved it by regular investing, debt avoidance, and prudent spending. Some never had lottery tickets, inheritance, or six-figure earnings. This is excellent news for Americans who have given up hope that they will ever amass significant wealth over their lifetime.

Many people think others use some magic method to become wealthy. How typical millionaires became wealthy would shock or amaze the ordinary person because some assume that millionaires only come from metropolitan areas. Holding onto these misconceptions could be what's keeping many people in poverty.

Millionaires engage in risky businesses. The underlying presumption of this myth is that millionaires acquire their status by investing all their resources in high-risk ventures. So, they became wealthy after those investments started to prosper. This isn't always the case—wealthy people take calculated risks and also diversify their investments.

Typical millionaires employ the same financial tools average individuals use to grow their money. Real estate and index funds are their two most popular investments. Many millionaires store their money in traditional assets, but some may include a few risky investments in their portfolio (Rose, 2019).

While accepting some risk is important when aspiring to become a millionaire, weighing profit versus danger is a constant consideration. Successful millionaires avoid making irrational investments, hoping to become wealthy. They start by carefully evaluating their options—perhaps this is why successful investors make adequate findings before prioritizing one asset over the other.

Millionaires simply receive inheritances. This might be the most prevalent millionaire myth today. Many people believe millionaires are trust fund kids who sit back and make ends meet with their parents' savings. Although many tv shows depict people gaining wealth via inheritance, this is not always the case in real life.

The vast majority (79%) of millionaires living in the United States inherited nothing from their parents or other relatives. While twenty-one percent of millionaires (or one in every five you see) may receive some inheritance, only three percent of those inherited $1 million or more. In actuality, most millionaires didn't come from wealthy families. According to the report, eight of every ten millionaires are from low-income or lower-middle-class families. Only 2% of millionaires questioned by Ramsey Solutions claimed to have wealthy parents (Ramsey Solutions, 2022).

The belief that they must be born wealthy has prevented many people from accomplishing their goals. After considering their lives, they conclude they cannot survive without help. Seventy-nine percent of today's millionaires, according to studies, did not get any inheritance—they worked hard until they achieved success (Mawer, 2022). They also have the tenacity to work toward their financial objectives and a strong understanding of monetary value from a young age.

Millionaires earn substantial incomes. Doctors, business owners, and senior executives would top your list if you were told to guess the professions most likely to create millionaires. The salary for those positions is fairly substantial, which is undoubtedly helpful. You would be surprised none of those positions made the list's top spot. Engineer, accountant, and teacher were the top three occupations mentioned by those 10,000 millionaires when asked what they did for a living (Ramsey Solutions, 2022).

Many millionaires work as teachers, even though they are severely underpaid. Teachers might understand the value of putting in significant effort and making long-term plans more than the average person.

Check these hard facts about self-made millionaires (Ramsey Solutions, 2022).

- Only sixty-nine percent of millionaires (or approximately seven out of ten wealthy people) had a household income of $100,000 or more.
- The average household income of one-third of millionaires was never over six figures.
- Millionaires holding senior leadership positions like CEO or CFO are just fifteen percent.
- Ninety-three percent of millionaires claimed they became wealthy through hard labor, not high wages.

What counts when becoming a millionaire is what you do with what you have, not how much cash you make. Someone who spends every dollar they earn is left with nothing to save or invest. How will they create wealth?

Millionaires happen to be in the right location at the appropriate time. Maybe someone said they wish they had traded crypto earlier or Bezos was fortunate to start Amazon when there were no rivals.

These expressions or beliefs send the message that wealthy people are just fortunate. Yet, if you examine the world's wealthiest individuals, you'll notice a distinct pattern. Individuals like Musk, Bezos, and Buffett began with the remarkable capacity to transform something small—money, an idea, or a vision—into something that adds value to millions of lives (Mawer, 2022).

Reports showed that eighty percent (or eight out of ten) of millionaires contributed to the 401(k) plan of their business, and that straightforward move was crucial to their financial success. Also, seventy-five percent of millionaires (or three out of four) claimed that their success was because of their long history of steady, routine investing (Ramsey Solutions, 2022).

Millionaires lead lavish lives. When you think about millionaires, you might imagine wealthy people living in opulent mansions and driving pricey sports cars. You will be surprised that your next-door neighbors are millionaires even though they travel in Volvo and Honda cars—they enjoy the content and economical lifestyles (Tardy, 2016).

Some millionaires spend their cash on essentials and a few items dear to them. When you consider the extravagant lifestyles of reality TV stars and social media influencers, believing or reaching the conclusion that millionaires favor lavish lifestyles is easy. But have you taken your time to study most millionaires?

Ninety-four percent of millionaires Ramsey Solutions surveyed lived on less money than they earn. Nearly three-quarters of the millionaire respondents claim never to have had a credit card balance! Furthermore, these millionaires affirmed that their monthly restaurant expenditure is $200 or less.

Ninety-three percent of millionaires always or occasionally use coupons when they purchase. Also, thirty-one percent of millionaires don't drive a fancy vehicle; instead, they drive a Honda or Toyota car (Ramsey Solutions, 2022).

Millionaires went to prestigious Ivy-league schools. You might be surprised to learn that fifteen percent of the Forbes 400 wealthiest individuals, all millionaires, do not even possess a high school diploma (Rose, 2019).

Ivy League degrees are only earned by a small percentage of millionaires, according to studies. In reality, sixty-two percent of millionaires have degrees from public universities, while ten percent have never attended college. Having a college education is beneficial since eighty-eight percent of millionaires, compared to thirty-three percent of the overall population surveyed by Ramsey Solutions, have a bachelor's degree. Still, education is not the only element determining financial success or the ability to accumulate money (Ramsey Solutions, 2022).

The truth is that millionaires have a variety of educational backgrounds. The wrong mindset might be the factor preventing some people from becoming financially free (or attaining millionaire status). The odds are in our favor if we let go of these false notions and acknowledge that gaining wealth demands endurance, bravery, discipline, and moving outside of our comfort zone.

DON'T LET THESE MISCONCEPTIONS HOLD YOU BACK

Some think there are magical means for becoming wealthy (but that's not true). A typical person would be shocked after realizing how millionaires acquired their wealth. That's because many people feel millionaires live or come from influential metropolitan business centers. But holding onto those millionaire misconceptions can keep you in poverty.

Are you aware that you'll never become a millionaire if you don't think you can? Believing in and acting on the millionaire myths can prevent you from becoming wealthy or reaching your financial goals. Believing the fallacies about wealth and the wealthy or holding onto even one of them can undermine your wealth-building efforts (Roomer, n.d.).

Accepting the millionaire misconceptions may trigger some (or all) of these problems.

Discouragement and lack of motivation. When individuals believe that becoming a millionaire is only achievable through means outside their control, such as inheriting wealth or winning the lottery, they may feel disempowered and give up on their financial goals.

Paying off a $50,000 debt when heavily in debt or having a negative net worth is tough to rationalize and deal with. Feeling discouraged or lacking motivation makes your aim of having a $1 million net worth seem beyond your grasp.

Motivation is crucial because you are engaging in more strenuous activities than you are accustomed to. You are undertaking an arduous task and acting in a non-comfortable manner. What makes the difference between individuals who accumulate riches and those putting things off (or making excuses) is motivation.

You can overcome many obstacles preventing you from accomplishing your goals if you have a strong will to succeed.

Poor financial decision-making. Adopting a *get-rich-quick* mentality rather than focusing on building wealth through consistent and intelligent financial planning can lead to poor financial decision-making and missed opportunities for growth and stability.

Consequences of poor financial decisions include bad credit scores, lack of savings, and dependence on debt. Also, making a poor financial decision may restrict your access to credit cards and loans with favorable rates and terms and leave you more vulnerable to monetary difficulties (Kilroy, 2022).

Poor financial choices can result in poor financial habits if not appropriately corrected or managed. For example, if you don't set aside money for emergencies, you might have to use your credit card to pay for a sizable unforeseen expense, which could trap you in a vicious cycle of high-interest debt.

You can recover from poor financial decisions by identifying your mistakes and developing a reasonable strategy to deal with the issue going forward.

Limiting beliefs. The ideas keeping you from realizing your full potential and restricting your view of what is possible are limiting beliefs (Finance Over Fifty, n.d.). These ideas, which are frequently deeply ingrained in your subconscious, serve as a lens through which you evaluate your experiences and assess your potential.

We all hold certain beliefs—they are formed early in life as a result of the experiences we have with our parents, families, peers, the media, and many other influences. They initially start as neutral conditions or facts in our lives.

These conditions mold our experiences, which in turn help our brains generate ideas and search for deeper meaning. We then use this information to interpret the events of our lives based on our feelings (Finance Over Fifty, n.d.).

The realities we accept as facts — even when they are not — are ultimately shaped by these interpretations, which influence our beliefs. And as we age, these convictions become more ingrained in our minds until they dominate all of our thoughts. Our behaviors are determined by the sensations that these thoughts inspire.

But these assumptions are often incorrect and simply undermine our efforts to lead satisfying lives. Our subsequent actions act as self-fulfilling obstacles that prevent us from achieving the goals we most want.

Believing that only specific backgrounds or education can lead to becoming a millionaire can limit individuals' potential and prevent them from pursuing their financial goals and reaching their full financial potential.

Missed opportunities for growth and stability. By not taking control of their finances, individuals may forfeit opportunities for growth and stability through savings and investments, sticking to a budget, and making smart financial decisions.

High-net-worth CEOs and others who have previously worked for themselves may encounter issues as they begin their financial planning process. Despite making a high income, people frequently miss out on financial opportunities because they don't have retirement planning (Choice Wealth, n.d.).

It's simple to believe that their retirement plan will be a success, and it often is, but a high income often hides the fact that once a job is over, there will probably be a shortfall. Similar to people with ordinary incomes, those who don't start saving early on may end up with insufficient funds for retirement.

Retirement means being independent for many Americans. When retirees have enough money saved to select when and how they want to retire, flexible retirements are preferred because they allow them to work, volunteer, or do anything they enjoy.

High-earning entrepreneurs and executives focus on using their businesses as retirement funds to subsidize them (for the rest of their life). It won't be known until the sale event takes place whether the sale of their business will cover their whole retirement (Choice Wealth, n.d.).

Suppose a business liquidation event occurs at the wrong time. In that case, many self-employed executives might be forced to invest all increased income in the business rather than in a retirement savings plan. It's uncommon for a business sale to occur at a high valuation or during a prime period; instead, it often occurs through an unfavorable incident that the executive was not prepared for.

The executive or owner continues to believe they can make it up later when dealing with financial planning and retirement plans since they overspend during the good times. Extra money is frequently invested in corporate expansion or personal extravagance rather than retirement savings during the good years (Choice Wealth, n.d.).

If you consistently organize your finances for retirement, a high income will allow you to save more and won't struggle to take advantage of opportunities for growth and stability. Don't pass up the chance to save for retirement now when you can.

Importance of recognizing and breaking free from the millionaire myths to achieve financial success

Anyone who develops or accepts the millionaire misconception may struggle to focus on their financial objectives or create wealth. They frequently think there's little or nothing to do to change their narratives. For example, since they didn't come from wealthy homes, they give up on trying to build prosperity.

If you harbor any millionaire fallacies, breaking free requires recognizing them. Discovering the source of your problems can help you overcome them. You will be motivated to reach your financial objectives when you defeat the millionaire myths. You will spot and act on opportunities that improve your fortune. Most of the millionaires in this country started with similar families, jobs, and backgrounds to you.

Breaking free from these falsehoods can help you develop a beneficial money mindset. If you want to be financially free, your vision and thoughts must align.

The relationships you build may facilitate or undermine your efforts to break free from these myths. Someone who always relates to negative-thinking individuals may soon become one of them—examining the people in your life and ensuring they share your healthy aspirations can help.

Learning to take control of your finances and reach your financial potential

Perhaps you are caught in a debt cycle.

You make too little money to sustain your lifestyle or want to start saving money for a big purchase like a house or an investment.

You might need assistance to move forward with your goals.

There are many advantages to managing your funds— you can achieve notable objectives, lessen the likelihood of accruing credit card debt or permanently resolve your debt problems. Also, you can feel at ease knowing that you are ready for life emergencies.

Follow these standards to take charge of your finances permanently. Knowing how to put money to work can be challenging, although proper money management attracts several benefits. You will quickly know how to best allocate future bonuses, raises, and budget surpluses.

Analyze your position. Discover the state of your finances if you want to control them. Create a sound strategy by carefully examining your spending patterns, debt level, financial objectives, and how to achieve them.

When evaluating your financial position, you should:

- Note every debt you have, including the due date, interest rate, and balance owed.
- Record your expenses for 30 or more days to know where your cash is going.
- Pay close attention to how your spending aligns with your budget.
- Examine your financial objectives and determine if you are on track to meet them.
- Include savings in your possession list.

Doing all these will provide you with a broad overview of your financial situation, enabling you to determine whether any changes are necessary.

Adopt a savings and investment mindset. Having a positive attitude toward money is crucial since it could reduce stress and enhance your general well-being. It is also the initial step in achieving present and long-term financial stability (Cueto, 2022).

A beneficial money perspective can facilitate healthy financial patterns. If someone has difficulty ditching wasteful lifestyles or saving for retirement or emergencies, working on their mindset might help them improve their habits.

Envision triumph. The strategies successful athletes and people use can benefit you and your financial habits. For example, you can develop a healthy money mindset and achieve financial freedom by visualizing your success.

Have the desire to learn. Whether you choose to learn through doing, hearing, or reading, some straightforward financial gurus freely impart their knowledge online. Regularly taking in this kind of information can improve your financial practices.

There are a variety of resources accessible to improve your money mindset, ranging from personal finance websites to budgeting spreadsheets for excellent money habits. Be sure to revisit any of your favorites, as you will likely have a new perspective on the same ideas after your budgeting skills grow.

Access your accounts regularly. Check the balances of your credit cards, personal loans, and bank accounts daily. Organize your invoices, expenses, and incoming revenue in a spreadsheet.

Doing this helps you avoid unpleasant surprises, lessen your stress level, and begin each day with a clear financial picture.

You will be able to make better selections and adopt a helpful money mindset with the aid of this short and simple exercise.

Evaluate each choice. Although it might seem obsessive, every choice you make can affect your financial future.

Setting up a budget can assist you in making wise financial decisions. For example, when you know that following your budget will leave you with a specific amount to put into your savings account, you'll wonder whether you need to spend more money on luxuries.

Prioritize saving over spending. Savings are not the last thing on the budget for those with excellent money habits and healthy money mindsets. Prioritize your savings objectives and make necessary adjustments for the rest of your life.

Do you wish to start an emergency fund, purchase a home or car, or go on that dream vacation?

Prioritize monthly contributions to those savings goals, then make a list of all your fixed debt payments before determining how much money is still available for takeout and discretionary spending.

Combine your debts. Developing better money habits is essential to living a happier life. You might still be weighing the consequences of prior errors.

Debt consolidation can have considerable monetary and mental benefits, including a monthly installment and a reduction in interest rates (Cueto, 2022).

A financial advisor can guide you through all these.

Follow a spending program. Plan for both immediate and future needs by controlling your expenditures.

Planning is the key to effective money management. If you are still determining how much of your income is disposable, it is simple to let your spending spiral out of control.

If you have a solid budget to fall back on each month, you will feel more confident knowing that you are in control of your finances.

The ability to plan major purchases without fearing that you'll miss the mark is possible by working toward a purpose and planning for the future. If you maintain your budget, you will be one step closer to reaching your financial objectives and saving money (Cueto, 2022).

Prepare for emergencies. Ensure you keep some money saved up in case something unexpected happens, like your boiler breaks in the middle of winter or your oven breaking.

Careful budgeting can lessen the blow of unforeseen expenses. It ensures you have a reserve of funds to draw from when you need them most.

During emergencies and despite your best efforts, you might need to take a loan or use your credit card to make ends meet. When taking out a loan, it is crucial to have a solid grasp of the amount you could repay monthly.

It will be necessary to follow your budget to determine how much you can borrow comfortably and to ensure that your repayments are included in your regular outgoings.

Make smart financial decisions. Someone's capacity to make sound financial decisions influences their ability to weigh options and make well-informed decisions about their financial situations. These decisions include when and how to save or spend, price comparison before making a large purchase, and planning for retirement or other long-term savings.

Increasing your savings and moving toward your financial goals both require making wise financial decisions. These decisions—no matter how minor or important—can affect your life. For example, you can increase your wealth and credit score by consistently making wise decisions like paying off your credit card monthly.

Understanding your financial goals is the first step in making wise financial decisions. There's a strong likelihood that you have some goals for your future, whether they involve retiring early, traveling the world, or accumulating wealth to donate to charities.

Don't just focus on the short-term effects of your financial decisions—take their extensive results into account instead. For example, it's simple to focus only on enjoyment if you use your credit card to pay for a vacation. You might even promise yourself you will pay off the debt soon.

But will a vacation loan limit your ability to make future payments? Are there greater chances that this will result in more debt?

The regular payments may force you to put off achieving other objectives, like accumulating money for a down payment on a house.

Evaluate the consequences of your actions before deciding.

You may be reading this book later in life, unable to take full advantage of the time value of money from when you are 18. This does not mean you can't achieve your goals; it only means your path is different. Empower yourself to achieve financial success, regardless of your background or starting point. Having dispelled some common myths surrounding millionaires, it's time to explore the practical strategies to become a millionaire yourself.

6

WHO WANTS TO BE A MILLIONAIRE?

"Most people fail to realize that in life, it's not how much money you make; it's how much money you keep."

— ROBERT T. KIYOSAKI

Being financially secure helps you accomplish more in life. Thanks to money and financial independence, you can explore the world, do new things, and live fully. This chapter outlines practical steps toward becoming a millionaire, highlights the benefits of utilizing retirement accounts, and emphasizes the significance of being intentional with your money.

SO YOU WANT TO BE A MILLIONAIRE

While some financial gurus think you need $1,000,000 to retire comfortably, everything depends on your lifestyle and perception of a pleasant life (Halimi, 2022). Individuals from wealthy backgrounds may not consider this a lofty ambition.

Becoming a millionaire might seem like a distant fantasy to people with regular employment or those barely surviving on their salaries. If you fall under this category, understanding compound interest and prioritizing saving or investing can help you reach your millionaire goal.

You may achieve $1 million by the end of your career if you plan well, have patience, and save wisely. Becoming a millionaire does not mean you must have a family fortune or a six-figure job. All that is required is budgeting your money carefully and starting to save early (Palmer, 2022).

Following these saving tips can ease your millionaire journey.

Make early savings. Starting early is the best approach to increasing your savings. You can benefit from compounding by doing this.

Suppose you are 20 years old. You would have a total investment of $240,000 if you contributed $500 to an IRA monthly for 40 years.

Assuming the contribution attracted a 7% return, your investment would increase to over $1.37 million (thanks to compound interest).

Limit debt and wasteful spending. Quit shopping sprees. Consider these before tapping your card:

Have I got a need for this?

Do I already possess something comparable?

Do I crave this more than becoming a millionaire?

Spending money on needless things takes money away from investments.

Consider this—you would earn $277,693, investing an extra $25 weekly for 40 years (based on the previous example) if you could eliminate $25 in wasteful spending from your weekly budget.

Save fifteen percent of earnings. The personal savings rate is the post-spending-and-taxation income percentage. The rate decreased to 2.3% in October 2022.

Experts say that's insufficient for retirement savings, let alone for those aiming to become millionaires (Palmer, 2022).

Think of saving at least 20% of your salary as savings, which includes money for retirement and emergency funds.

Get extra income. My wife and I worked second jobs for a while to start our debt payment journey. This gave us the capacity we needed to begin our fortune journey. In the age we live in today, it has never been easier to find another source of income. Countless apps will get you paid for running errands or doing chores for others that can be done on your way home from work or on a day off.

It will be challenging to become a millionaire if your income is insufficient to save 15% of it. Consider making these choices:

- Asking for a raise.
- Working more time.
- Taking up a second job.

If your financial objective is to become a millionaire, that extra cash you receive each year might help you achieve it.

Avoid embracing lifestyle inflation. Don't succumb to the pressure to increase your standard of living if you are interested in becoming a millionaire.

Getting a raise or earning extra cash from a side business does not mean your expenses should increase.

Spending less helps increase savings and investments; don't assume that you can spend more because you make more. As your income increases, try to increase your personal savings rate.

Get assistance when necessary. Retirement planning may be stressful because there are so many investment options and emergencies to plan for. For example, sixty percent of employees admitted to having anxiety about retirement preparation. Also, only 25% of Americans feel confident that they are taking the steps to prepare for retirement (Palmer, 2022). That is why seeking professional help is so crucial.

Working with a certified financial advisor is helpful unless you are a financial hero. They may assist you with setting financial objectives, creating a budget, and selecting investments.

Develop yourself. My wife and I went back to school to get our MBAs after we were debt free and finished it without debt to increase our yearly earnings. This process, like saving, is a slow and steady one. Graduating with a new certificate or degree doesn't entitle you to more earnings automatically.

Putting money into your development is one of the best investments you'll ever make.

Gaining new knowledge and skills might prepare you for potential jobs and obstacles. By enrolling in classes, make it your mission to master a new skill every three months.

Developing yourself doesn't even need to be major changes or obstacles. You can improve yourself and your organization by outlining or planning your week. Consider getting a desk calendar and jotting down your weekly activities on it. This ensures that your actions or appointments are visually displayed for your convenience.

Get a planner and create a daily routine in it to accomplish this. You can make a timetable using an app on your mobile device.

Develop relationships both inside and outside of the office by networking. Making connections is crucial for developing your career because it may lead to more excellent opportunities. Make an effort to go to professional or industry events to network.

Get a mentor—they may help and motivate you to reach your goals and attempt new things, like applying for various jobs or forming new routines. Your mentor may assist you in achieving your objectives with methods that are workable for you. They may develop an action plan for you to do this.

Try seeking a mentor in your workplace or even at a networking event. You might also think about working with a career coach.

You can advance professionally and establish side hustles that provide passive money by honing your abilities. Also, improving your financial thinking and understanding empowers you to make wiser financial decisions to improve your prospects.

Maintaining your physical and mental health is also essential. Financial independence is great, but living the millionaire lifestyle is challenging if your physical and mental health deteriorates.

A word on retirement savings accounts

Can compound interest make me wealthy? Your investment level will determine this. But compound interest can lead you to financial success faster than simple interest.

Suppose you save $5 daily into an account that earns 8% interest. You'll have more than $1 million in assets after 50 years.

If you have access to any employer-based retirement plans, use them. Your savings will benefit from an additional boost since many employers match some employees' contributions.

The previous chapter showed some millionaires credit their workplace retirement savings plans for wealth.

What is the impact of saving and investing early on the ability to retire early?

If you are in your 20s, you might think retirement is so far away. This reason is why many people do not invest in their future. Anybody who is getting close to retirement will tell you how quickly the years pass and how tough it is to start saving for retirement early (Richmond, 2022)

Also, as time goes on, you will incur expenses you don't have now, like a mortgage and a family. You may not make much money as you start a job, but you have enough time to create wealth if you make retirement contributions.

Retirement saving becomes a far more enjoyable—and exciting—prospect when you have time. Setting away money may significantly influence your future, especially when you're still paying off your student loans. You can design your retirement strategy, but if you lack the expertise, an investment advisor can help you achieve your objectives.

Importance of having a retirement plan and attaining financial stability during retirement years

The goal of planning is to ensure a regular income after retirement. Your retirement plan's effectiveness depends on your ultimate objective, revenue, and age.

Getting older can be expensive—while unnecessary spending may decrease, medical costs will rise. Stress and worry can result from not having sufficient money to cover future obligations, especially when inflation is taken into account (Franklin Templeton, n.d.).

Having a retirement investing strategy will allow you to maintain your financial independence in your later years.

Here are the top reasons for creating a retirement plan:

Retirement benefits. Even if pensions exist, they might not be enough to pay for every retirement need. This makes building a balanced retirement strategy that includes fixed-income and mutual fund assets essential.

Financial freedom. Older adults have relied on their children for retirement support for years. Young people are becoming more independent recently—they frequently can't financially support their parents.

Even if they can, being in charge of your own affairs will give you more freedom to live your life however you choose because no one else will hold you accountable.

Increasing costs. While making retirement plans, inflation is an essential factor to consider. You might have to lower your standard of living if you need to keep up with the price increases.

Health emergencies. The expense of healthcare is essential to comprehending the significance of retirement planning.

- Healthcare inflation is increasing startlingly rapidly while retail costs are steadily rising.
- Health, unlike other financial objectives, cannot be negotiated.

Retirement investment platforms to consider when building financial stability include:

Retirement Plans

Employer-sponsored retirement plans are sometimes perceived as being somewhat generic. Yet, there are many other kinds of methods, some of which are inexpensive and can speed up the process of saving for retirement.

Which one you should pick will depend on your employer and the industry in which they operate. Sometimes, an employer will match your savings to a certain proportion (Mercadante, 2023).

401(k)

This is the most prevalent employer-sponsored retirement plan, and large for-profit companies are the leading providers.

The employee has absolute authority over the funds after retirement and decides which investments to place their money in under the 401(k) plan. Additionally, the tax deduction for employee contributions is available in the year of the grant.

Following retirement, the employee will receive distributions subject to ordinary income tax. The assets can be rolled over into a standard IRA, or the 401(k) plan of another company without being taxed or subject to early withdrawal penalties should the employee decide to withdraw the money before retirement.

Any money taken out but not transferred to another qualifying plan is subject to income tax payment and a 10% withdrawal fee if withdrawn before retirement. The maximum yearly contribution for 2023 is $22,500. A catch-up option that permits extra contributions of $7,000 for 2023 is available to employees who are 50 years or older (Mercadante, 2023).

403(b)

Except for being created for charitable organizations, the 403(b) plan is nearly identical to a 401(k). In addition to associations, this retirement investment applies to public school systems, hospitals, home healthcare providers, and welfare assistance providers.

The majority of the plans' funding comes from employee contributions, which are deductible from income when made. Employers may contribute a specified amount in matching donations. Contribution limitations are the same as those of 401(k) plans, and investment returns grow tax-deferred (Mercadante, 2023).

457

State and local government employees can contribute to the 457 retirement scheme, and the program functions much like the 401(k) plans. In other words, their functionality and contribution caps are the same as those of 401(k) plans.

If a company provides a 401(k) and a 457 plan, the employee may contribute to both programs, doubling the 401(k) plan's contribution cap. In 2023, a participant could contribute to each totaling $22,500.

Traditional and Roth IRAs

Saving for retirement and reducing taxes are possible with individual retirement accounts (IRAs). These accounts are primarily intended for independent contractors. Traditional and Roth IRAs have several significant differences, although sharing many of the same objectives.

You can make pre-tax contributions to a regular IRA. In addition to saving money for retirement, this lowers your taxable income for the year. As soon as you take out the money, taxes become owed.

You may contribute after-tax money to a Roth IRA. Taxes are not saved immediately, but after retirement, the money you invested and the income it generates are tax-free.

Traditional IRA contributions can reduce your annual taxable income. You may be eligible for extra tax advantages such as educational loan deductions or the tax credit for kids by lowering your adjusted gross income (AGI).

You will be subject to taxes and an early withdrawal penalty of 10% if you take money from a regular IRA before turning 59½ (Appleby, 2023). In some limited cases, such as when you use the funds to cover eligible first-time homebuyer expenses, you can prevent the fines (but not the taxes). The penalty may not apply to permanent disability or a particular amount of unpaid medical expenditures.

There is no tax deduction available for contributions to a Roth IRA. The Roth IRA withdrawals you make in retirement are tax free. You have no extra dues because you paid the entire tax payment beforehand.

Restrictions on income eligibility apply to Roth IRAs. Individual contributions will phase down starting at $129,000 for singles in 2022 and must be less than their modified AGI of $144,000. To contribute to a Roth, married couples must have adjusted AGIs under $214,000 (Appleby, 2023).

RMDs (required minimum distributions) are not required for Roth IRAs, so you are not obligated to take any distributions at any time throughout your lifetime or at any age. Roth IRAs are perfect vehicles for wealth transfer because of this attribute.

Although distributions must be made or the account must be rolled over into a new IRA, beneficiaries of Roth IRAs are not subject to income tax on withdrawals.

Simplified Employee Pension (SEP) and SIMPLE IRAs

A SEP IRA is just like a regular individual retirement account. Business owners can contribute tax-deductible money to SEP IRAs. Until payouts are made in retirement, investments grow tax free.

With a regular IRA, you can contribute up to $6,500 in 2023 and $6,000 in 2022. You may increase your contribution by $1,000 per year if you are 50 years old or older. With a SEP IRA, you can save up to $61,000 in 2022 and $66,000 in 2023, over ten times that amount (O'Shea, 2023).

Employees 21 years of age or older working with an employer for at least three of the last five years, and earning at least $650 in 2022 or $750 in 2023, are eligible to take part. You would have to pay a contribution on behalf of an employee for the 2023 plan year, for instance, if they earned $850 while working for you in 2019, 2020, and 2021 (O'Shea, 2023).

SIMPLE IRA

Most small firms with 100 employees or fewer can use a SIMPLE IRA as their retirement savings plan. A non-elective contribution from the employer of up to 2% of the employee's pay is an option, as is a dollar-for-dollar match of the staff's contributions of up to 3% of the employee's salary (Kagan, 2021).

SIMPLE IRAs are appealing since they only need initial plan paperwork and yearly employee disclosures in terms of paperwork. The plan is created by the employer and is managed by a financial institution.

Starting and operating costs are modest, and businesses can deduct contributions from their taxes to support their workforce. The employer must employ 100 or fewer people to be qualified to create a SIMPLE IRA.

Self-employed individuals or single proprietors can create a SIMPLE IRA. Employees must have received at least $5,000 in pay in each of the last two calendar years to be eligible to take part in the plan. They must also anticipate receiving at least $5,000 in salary this year (Kagan, 2021).

Companies may choose more lenient participation criteria if they so choose. Employees who get union benefits may be excluded by their employer from membership.

Taxable Brokerage Accounts

A brokerage account is a licensed investment account housed in a brokerage business (Chen, 2023). When an investor transfers money into their brokerage account, the brokerage company executes orders on their behalf for securities like mutual funds, bonds, stocks, and ETFs (exchange-traded funds).

Investors own the assets in their investment accounts, and as a result, they are typically required to report the income they receive from the accounts as taxable. They have the option to choose the model that best meets their financial needs from a variety of brokerage accounts and brokerage company kinds.

In exchange for high fees, some full-service brokers offer in-depth investing advice and other services. On the opposite end of the pay scale, most internet brokers merely provide a safe interface via which clients can place trade orders. For this service, they impose comparatively modest prices.

Digital platforms called robo-advisors provide investment and financial planning services run by algorithms rather than individuals. They rarely cost much and have modest minimum opening balance requirements (Chen, 2023).

Brokerage accounts may vary in terms of the ability for investors to trade on margin to a certain extent, the speed at which orders are executed, analytical tools available, and the range of tradable assets.

Brokerage accounts have categories—they are:

Full-service account. Investors seeking financial advice may want to investigate full-service brokerage houses like Merrill, Morgan Stanley, or Wells Fargo Advisors (Chen, 2023).

Financial advisors are compensated for providing their clients with investment planning help, transaction execution, market and investment monitoring, and other services. They can operate conditionally, where trades don't need prior client consent, or a non-discretionary basis, where customers must approve all transactions.

Either trading commissions or adviser fees are charged for full-service brokerage accounts. Whether the advice came from the customer or the advisor, and regardless of whether the trade was profitable, a commission account produces a charge whenever an investment is purchased or sold.

A flat annual cost for an adviser fee account can be anywhere between 0.5% and 2% of the overall account amount (Chen, 2023). No commissions apply to the purchase or sale of investments in return for this fee. Financial advisers and investors should discuss remuneration structures as soon as a relationship is established.

Discount account. Investors who enjoy using a hands-off bargaining strategy may opt for a cheap brokerage company. Compared to their full-service competitors, these companies charge much-reduced fees. These types of accounts are generally not intended for the less experienced client.

In exchange for these cheaper fees, inexpensive brokerage firms provide fewer services. This, however, might be advantageous for investors who are primarily focused on controlling costs and carrying out trades through user-friendly internet trading platforms (Chen, 2023). For example, an investor choosing a standard discount broker can expect to deposit at least $500 to start a standard taxable brokerage account (or retirement account).

Most stocks, options, and ETFs have low or no commission fees when bought or sold. While this varies from broker to broker, some cheap brokers may impose commissions for lightly traded or non-US equities.

Government bond purchases usually don't come with commissions, but bonds sold on the secondary market might. Several brokers, such as Fidelity and Schwab, also provide an extensive selection of mutual funds with no transaction fees (Chen, 2023).

Robo-Advisor. Robo-advisory accounts are those where the investments are chosen by algorithms and without the involvement of a human, not the account holder. Additionally, those investments are often limited to ETFs or mutual funds. The expense may equal 0.25 percent of assets under management (AUM) annually (Chen, 2023).

A minimum deposit of $10, $500, $5,000, or more may be needed to start an account. Both novice and seasoned investors who choose a hands-off approach to portfolio management may benefit from using robo-advisors.

As you save cash and need to transfer it to one of these investment accounts, it is critical to understand where your money is going and who is in charge of watching it for you. The risk of losing money can vary significantly between these accounts. As you learn the different types of accounts and gain an understanding of what your money needs to do for you, it is generally best to start with accounts from your employer or more generic mutual funds that target a retirement year. These accounts will have someone available to answer questions, limited risk, and modest fees associated with them.

How can you make a million dollars?

Your decisions today will significantly affect where you end up years from now, even if you are unaware of them.

Reaching the million-dollar barrier is feasible, but it will require some effort. The best companion of a millionaire is compound growth, often known as compound interest. Your investment earnings are what matters.

In addition to the compound interest, you have the time necessary to build wealth since you're still young—this is also the edge you have over your parents and teachers. For example, based on the table below, you could accumulate $1 million in fewer than 38 years by saving $100 per week at an annual interest rate of 7.5%.

Weekly Contribution (USD)	10 Years Balance (USD)	20 Years Balance (USD)	30 Years Balance (USD)	40 Years Balance (USD)	50 Years Balance (USD)
50	38,030.90	116,413.78	277,963.38	610,922.20	1,297,160.85
100	76,060.04	232,822.20	555,913.94	1,221,816.21	2,594,261.82
250	190,150.99	582,058.17	1,389,791.26	3,054,554.63	6,485,684.49

Taking advantage of compound interest by beginning to save as early as possible can help you easily reach your goal of becoming a millionaire. Your interest earnings increase over time if you start saving early.

How much do you need to start your journey toward becoming a millionaire?

There is no set rule for how much money you need to start investing to become a millionaire. If you are younger, you can afford to save less initially as you have more time to build wealth and can handle more risk. However, if you delay saving until later, you must contribute more each month. Early and consistent saving or investing can help you attain financial freedom quickly. If you haven't started yet, could you set a monthly transfer to a savings account of $100 today? The first hurdle is just beginning. If you can start your savings today, work on your budget tomorrow and check to see if you have any surplus to move to savings at the beginning of next month.

BE INTENTIONAL

Being purposeful is committing to, concentrating on, and paying attention to something significant to you. You must be upfront and transparent regarding what you want to do if you desire to be deliberate each day. Next, you must take steps to make it happen.

This is a skill you can develop daily and one that can transform your life. Determining and acting on your priorities will be two guiding principles for moving your life ahead and making daily progress.

You can grow more conscious and accomplish more robust objectives in your company and personal life by being deliberate—this gives your day a distinct direction, order, and a good attitude.

Making a conscious decision to act on your priorities is crucial to learning to be purposeful. Living intentionally involves deciding to live the life you desire instead of letting other people control your thoughts, feelings, and behavior.

If you want to be intentional in life, following these tips should help.

Create and stick to a budget. You may plan to spend, accomplish goals, and prepare for operational changes using a budget.

Using a budget can help you break free from consumer culture (or avoid impulse buying). Your savings will improve when you are in control of your finances.

Make informed and deliberate spending decisions. People can gain more confidence in their decision-making if they make it with knowledge. Attending business classes or getting a coach may improve your financial knowledge and spending decisions.

Prioritize savings and investments. People may protect their finances and earn income by saving.

Regularly review and adjust your financial plan. By evaluating your budget, you better control your spending, boost your savings, and move closer to your long-term financial objectives. It's a crucial facet of personal finance and essential to effective money management.

Seek professional advice when necessary. Financial coaches frequently help their customers with the psychological and behavioral aspects of managing their finances. To develop a better attitude that results in improved financial habits, a coach can assist you in identifying the factors that influence your financial decisions.

Stay disciplined and avoid impulsive spending. Giving in to an impulse purchase won't help you reach your financial objectives, whether debt relief, home equity development, or retirement planning. Impulsive purchases and overspending will devour any excess cash you were saving to use toward those fantastic goals.

Be mindful of long-term financial stability rather than short-term gains. You have something to strive for when you have a long-term financial objective. It's simple to become mired in the day-to-day operations of a company and lose sight of the more comprehensive picture. A long-term goal keeps you focused and facilitates decision-making for your company's future.

Continuously educate yourself on personal finance and make informed decisions. One fundamental life skill that directly affects one's well-being is understanding finances. If taught young, fundamentals like debt, debt management, saving, and investing will provide a solid basis for money habits.

Set clear and achievable financial goals. Whatever strategy you have for your cash is considered a financial objective. Every area of your life should have plans, but clear financial objectives enable you to put your money where it can help achieve your objectives (Cruze, 2022).

How can you set clear, achievable financial goals?

Specify your objective. Overly ambiguous goals are one reason people fail to achieve them. You may wish to manage my finances better. How do you interpret that? Simplify it! What if you opt to deal with your debt instead? You should focus your money on that particular area specifically.

Let's now discuss how this objective might be further subdivided.

Set quantifiable objectives. You wish to eliminate your debt. Choose a precise amount at this point to measure your progress and determine whether you achieved your objective.

Dividing your ultimate debt-free goal into smaller objectives is a good idea. Hence, even before you begin, you will feel encouraged. For example, let's say your overall debt is $30,000, but you wish to start by paying off a $500 department store credit card. Well, that's an objective we can measure!

Set an end date. If your goals don't have a deadline, it's tempting to put them off. *Someday* is not one of the seven days that make up a week. Don't keep saying someday.

You must set a deadline for yourself that is both acceptable and moderately difficult. Reverting to the store credit card example, when do you wish to achieve your objective? $60 per month is what you'll need to spend if you want to pay it off in a year.

Can this work? Is this too long to wait?

Be sure these are your objectives. It's simple to observe what other people are doing and assume that you ought to follow suit. Do your neighbors have the newest models of vehicles? Does that one gal who posts on Instagram usually go on fancy vacations?

Hey, congrats to them! But, it does not follow that you must follow suit. We are playing a game we can never win when we evaluate ourselves with other people. Hence, be sure the financial goals you set are appropriate for you. You shouldn't take out a second mortgage simply because your friends are doing it for newly renovated kitchens.

Put on your blinders, concentrate on your lane, and run the race in your direction. And be specific about the reasons behind your objective selection.

Create a goal statement. Did you realize that setting objectives in writing will improve the likelihood that you will achieve them? What they say about writing things down is true, helping you focus on the task at hand. Now write down your objectives. After that, attach them to your desk, car, or bathroom mirror.

You can type them in the Notes application on your cell phone, take a screenshot, and then set it as your background image so that it appears when you pick up the device. You'll stay motivated and on track if your goals are visible.

You've learned the fundamental principles of saving and being intentional with your money; now it's time to take the next step in building wealth through investing. But where do you start? This next chapter will walk you through investing and explore creating a well-rounded investment portfolio.

7

INVESTING FOR GROWTH

"I will tell you how to become rich. Close the doors. Be fearful when others are greedy. Be greedy when others are fearful."

— WARREN BUFFETT

An enterprise may fail to provide income or lose value over time. A business in which you invest might fail. Your securities can lose value when you liquidate them. Your portfolio may not improve in the long run.

Listening to or believing these thoughts can prevent you from accumulating riches. This chapter emphasizes the significance of investing in wealth creation, discusses the critical factors to consider, and provides tips for constructing a diversified investment portfolio.

OVERVIEW OF INVESTING

Investing entails putting your cash to work by purchasing assets, like stocks or bonds, to produce profits (or returns) above your initial investment. When discussing investing, people frequently refer to financial markets—where investors buy and sell assets like stocks and bonds (Hayes, 2022).

A purchase made to earn more money is known as an investment. Appreciation occurs when an asset's value rises. When a person buys a product as an investment, they do not intend to use it immediately; instead, they plan to use it to make money later.

An investment usually uses a resource today—time, effort, money, or an asset—in anticipation of receiving a more significant return than what was first invested. A financial asset, for instance, might be bought by an investor now, hoping it would provide income later on or be sold for more money.

Investments are made to make money and build value over time. Every strategy for producing future income is an investment. This involves buying bonds, equities, or real estate. Another thing that can be viewed as an investment is buying a property that can be utilized to manufacture items.

Generally, any activity to generate extra income can also be considered an investment. This is why self-investment activities like expanding knowledge, enhancing abilities, and seeking further education are crucial to a person's overall development.

Importance of growing wealth

Opening an investment account is a successful strategy for investing money and increasing wealth. Your cash may see value growth that exceeds inflation if you make wise investment decisions.

Compounding's effectiveness and the risk-return trade-off are the main reasons for investing in higher growth potential. When earnings or dividends are generated by investment and then reinvested, compounding occurs —these profits or dividends produce additional yields.

Compounding is how your investments produce income from prior income (Wells Fargo, n.d.). For example, if you decide to reinvest dividends from a stock you purchased that pays dividends, do so to benefit from the compounding effect.

These are a few advantages of growing wealth through investing—you will:

Beat inflation. You will eventually lose money if you don't invest and raise your capital. Inflation is entirely responsible for this. While inflation rates fluctuate considerably, they have hovered around 3% on average (Farrington, 2023).

You will remain far ahead of inflation and grow the value of your money if you invest your cash and receive an average rate of return of seven percent.

Create wealth. If you are serious about increasing your wealth, you must develop an investing strategy that works for you and your objectives.

The wealthy make investments; the poor buy products.

Early retirement. Making your cash work for you can ensure you have enough to retire. Your ability to benefit from compound interest will increase as you invest more money. As the compounding effect grows, your ability to retire will get closer.

Reduce taxes. Your capacity to reduce your tax burden is another MASSIVE benefit of investing! For example, 401(k), SEP IRA, and Traditional IRAs are not subject to taxation in the contribution year (Farrington, 2023).

If you withdraw it during retirement, you must pay taxes on it. You will pay much less in taxes than the year you contributed, depending on your income level. You can use a retirement account like a Roth IRA if you prefer to pay your taxes now—this option allows you to pay taxes now and avoid paying any tax upon withdrawal. Most people would benefit from a combination of taxable assets based on their ages and income levels now and projected future earnings.

The ordinary income tax rates you would pay for a regular 9–5 job are substantially higher than capital gains tax rates, even in taxable accounts! These are just simple instances. The tax code contains a ton of loopholes that benefit investors. Thanks to this, the wealthy maintain their wealth while paying low taxes!

Speak with your CPA or financial advisor to develop a personalized investment strategy that would match your unique goals if you need to reduce your tax burden. One approach to assist you in improving your financial situation and achieving your long-term objectives is to build a portfolio of high-quality assets and steer clear of items you hear about in the rumor mills.

Impact of investing on overall financial stability and growth

Investing can play a critical role in reaching financial goals, such as retirement and becoming a millionaire, in several ways:

Long-term wealth accumulation. Investment returns can rise (appreciate) in value or produce income (interest or dividends). The interest and dividends you receive from investments can increase your wealth.

Your money can grow through investing over time, boosting your wealth, and assisting you in achieving your financial objectives.

Compound interest. Compound interest can be earned on your original investment and the accumulated value over time. By investing early and frequently, you can benefit from this.

It speeds up your money's growth because compound interest is computed on both the original principle and the value that has accrued.

The growth of the initial investments and the income from those investments, coupled because of compounding, can have a snowball effect.

Diversification. You can spread your risk among various investments by investing in multiple items or funds, which will help you diversify your portfolio and lessen the impact of market instability on your financial objectives.

If you put all of your cash into a single company's stock and it fell, you would likely lose part, if not all, of it. If the issuer of a bond you invested your whole savings in files for bankruptcy, you would also lose some, if not all, of your money.

By selecting various investments and investment kinds, diversification helps reduce the risk associated with such circumstances. Even in a decreasing market, diversification cannot ensure investment returns or remove the risk of loss altogether, but it does significantly limit it.

Long-term financial stability. In the long run, investing in a mix of low and high-risk assets, such as bonds and stocks, can offer stability and growth, assisting you in achieving your financial objectives and financial security in retirement.

Professional management. By investing in professionally managed funds, you can benefit from experience managing your money, which can help you achieve your financial objectives and maximize returns.

THE DIFFERENT INVESTMENT FLAVORS

Investing in real estate can be a tremendously lucrative hobby for many people. Keeping or holding your property for a long period makes its value appreciate.

It is also conceivable for things to go wrong and to lose your investment in this area. You know that to build wealth, you must have more than just a savings account; deciding how to use your funds can be highly perplexing. Choose the investment types and the solutions that will best meet your needs based on your tolerance for risk.

Before creating wealth, knowing the various investment possibilities and their advantages and disadvantages is a good idea.

Types of investments

You have many alternatives as an investor on where to invest your money. It is crucial to consider different investment types thoroughly.

Investors with common sense avoid putting all of their eggs in one basket. Instead, they become acquainted with a few distinct investment kinds and employ their understanding of each to profit in various ways.

There are many investment packages available. However, before investing money and assembling your portfolio, you must know all your alternatives. There are benefits and drawbacks to each sort of investment.

The ideal investments will rely on your risk appetite, market knowledge, the window of time to prevent short-term capital gains, and initial investment goals. Undoubtedly, a couple of the many available investment types will be successful for you, so let us get started.

Stocks. A share of ownership in a publicly listed corporation is what you purchase when you buy a stock. Stock markets allow investors to purchase stocks from companies. Businesses typically engage in this strategy to raise funds for expansion. The stock value naturally rises if they develop and succeed (Thrivent, 2022).

A fantastic way to create long-term wealth is through stocks. Still, because of their volatility and sensitivity to market changes, the value of your investment may decline even when the firm is performing well.

One of the most well-liked investment types is stocks. The terms stock market and equity market are interchangeable; thus, you might also see them referred to as equities. They provide the potential for big profits over the long term if you are ready to endure the ups and downs. Consider purchasing bonds or other assets to facilitate better financial stability.

Pros

- Stocks have a high risk but have an enormous potential return.
- Stocks often produce more significant returns than most other investment kinds over time.

Cons

- Stocks carry risk. Investing in stocks carries a high risk of financial loss, and you can almost certainly expect to experience losses for a while (Feeling Financial, n.d.).
- You have issues if you need your money back when your equities are declining.
- Investing in individual stocks can also take time and effort. The possibility of huge returns is alluring, but the reality is that stocks do not always go up, and many individuals have had unpleasant experiences investing in stocks.

Best uses

Long-term, risk-tolerant investors make the best stock investments.

Investments in a varied portfolio of stocks may be made by those who require and seek growth to accomplish their objectives. This will work if you can endure the ups and downs of your investments.

Bonds. A government or business borrows money when you purchase a bond. They offer to repay your loan with interest over a predetermined time in exchange for your loan.

Given their lower volatility than equities and complete faith and credit backing from the government or company issuing them, bonds are frequently considered safer investment options (Thrivent, 2022).

Although bonds offer stability, there are certain disadvantages to them. Compared to stocks, they frequently provide smaller returns. The value of your bond will also decrease if interest rates increase. Nevertheless, using bonds to diversify your portfolio and lower your total risk can be fantastic.

In the end, bonds are a more cautious investment best suited for buyers seeking a steady and dependable investment. To receive the bond's total value, you must wait until it matures. On the other hand, interest will be accrued as you go.

Pros

- Bonds have the potential to increase in value as well as generate income.
- They may be safer investments than stocks, depending on who issued the bond. The government of the United States is a reasonably secure bet to remain in operation and repay you; thus, bonds from this country are typically seen as relatively safe (Feeling Financial, n.d.). However, because junk bonds produced by financially precarious corporations are riskier, they typically have to pay higher interest rates.
- For those with high incomes, certain bonds offer tax-free income.

Cons

- Your use of a particular bond may have many drawbacks. Even though safe bonds may have a lower risk of losing money, they struggle to stay up with inflation.
- You likely want to put only some of your money into these kinds of assets if you are going to maximize your long-term development potential.

- Also, there is a danger that the bond issuer could go out of business, in which case neither your principal nor interest payments would be made.
- As interest rates fluctuate, even safe bonds can experience a loss of value, which is a nasty shock to cautious investors. Bond prices drop as interest rates increase.
- If you plan to keep a bond for a very long time, this is not a concern for you (although you will be locked with an investment that pays lower interest than you could elsewhere). You would lose money if forced to sell the bond before its maturity.

Best uses

Most frequently, bonds are employed to diversify a portfolio, provide income, and lower risk.

There is undoubtedly a place for some bonds, regardless of how much risk you wish to accept.

Funds—mutual funds and ETFs

Mutual funds. Mutual funds invest the money collected from many investors in various securities. Professional money managers that manage mutual funds decide which assets to put in the fund. Investors can benefit from diversity, liquidity, and expert management through mutual funds.

Compared to alternative investment options, mutual funds often charge more outstanding fees. However, compared to what you would spend as an individual investor, you can have cheaper expenses overall when buying in mutual funds (Thrivent, 2022). That is because skilled fund managers allocate your portfolio wisely, sparing you from conducting research and making judgment calls on responding to market and economic conditions.

Mutual funds can be a terrific method to invest in various securities without researching. Furthermore, mutual funds are available for every goal, including stock, bond, and mixed-asset funds. You can pick a fund that fits your investment objectives and risk tolerance, regardless of your investing experience.

ETFs. Mutual funds and exchange-traded funds are comparable in many ways. Additionally, ETFs combine funds from many investors and invest them in various securities. Nonetheless, they can be purchased and sold all day because they trade on an exchange like stocks. ETFs frequently charge less in fees than mutual funds do (Thrivent, 2022).

While ETFs may have sales commission fees associated with each purchase, these may still be less expensive than mutual fund fees. However, ETFs can be highly volatile and susceptible to changes in the market. Using ETFs may allow you to invest in various assets without researching.

Pros

- Using mutual funds and ETFs allows you to effortlessly diversify (or distribute your money over multiple investments) by making it simple to do so with just one fund.
- You can save time and cash on transaction fees because you don't have to handle everything yourself.
- Despite their flaws, target date funds make it simple to diversify with just one investment (Feeling Financial, n.d.).

Cons

- There are a few drawbacks to these kinds of funding. Most issues arise from the sort of fund you select or the particular fund you may use.
- Knowing what you are getting is crucial because funds might be pricey or poorly

managed. While some take less risk, others are hazardous.
- Mutual funds can occasionally result in tax surprises, although those occurrences are unlikely for someone beginning from scratch and investing a few hundred dollars monthly.

Best uses

Mutual funds make terrific investments in the long run. They allow you to select an investment kind and delegate the administration to another party.

They are frequently used to plan for retirement and other long-term objectives.

Investment trusts. Another category of pooled investment is trusts. One of the most well-known types of securities in this group is real estate investment trusts (REITs).

REITs engage in residential or commercial real estate, and from the rental revenue generated by these properties, they regularly distribute money to their investors (Picardo, 2022).

Because of their stock exchange trading, REITs benefit their investors from immediate liquidity.

Real estate. It may be exciting and rewarding to make investments in property. Leverage is a simple way to purchase a property where a down payment is made, and the remaining balance is paid over time.

Once the paperwork is signed, you can start making money off the property. You can buy a house outright, rent it out, sell it after remodeling, or invest in REITs.

Pros

- Unlike stocks and bonds, which fluctuate in value over time, real estate tends to rise in value over time.
- Your rental properties can generate a reliable passive income for you.
- Leverage can increase your ability to profit from your assets when appropriately applied.
- It is among the simplest investing forms to comprehend.

Cons

- It ranks among the most expensive investment options.
- Leverage may result in losing money on your house if values fall dramatically.

- Real estate is difficult to sell and takes a long time to sell. When an emergency arises, they might need to sell more quickly.
- You must spend a lot of money to keep your property in good shape. Taxes, agency commissions, and maintenance costs must be paid.

Alternative investments. The alternative energy sector is expanding and getting more complicated every day.

Investing in something that performs differently from stocks and bonds or aids you in achieving a specific goal is the fundamental concept behind alternatives.

Alternatives may include investing in foreign currencies, precious metals, commodities, and properties (Feeling Financial, n.d.).

Pros

- Alternatives provide you the opportunity to create another income stream.
- They would generate returns independent of market conditions or at least a profit while your equities are losing money.
- Alternatives contribute to portfolio diversification. They provide more

opportunities for risk management, capital growth, and income generation.
- They offer more protection than stocks and bonds against specific risks (such as inflation or a depreciating dollar).

Cons

- Alternatives may be complex—they may surprise investors by moving more quickly than you would expect because of the difficulty in understanding them.
- Investments of this nature are traded in potentially very volatile markets.
- Alternatives can cost more money, depending on which ones you use and how you learn about them.

Best uses

Adding alternatives might help a portfolio become more diversified and complete.

Putting too much money into any alternative investment is usually not a good idea. Long-term investors might find having a small amount of exposure beneficial.

Options and derivatives. Financial derivatives get their worth from another product, such as a stock or an index.

Popular derivatives allow customers to purchase or sell assets at a predetermined window of time without being obligated to do so. Because derivatives frequently use leverage, they are high-risk, high-reward investments (Picardo, 2022).

Commodities. Examples include currencies, metals, oil, grains, and animal goods.

ETFs or commodity futures—contracts to commit to buying or selling a particular quantity at a certain price on a given date in the future—can be used to trade them. Both hedging risk and speculation can be done with commodities.

Choosing the right type of investment

Consider your style. You may consider these factors when choosing an investment.

Active vs. passive. Active management of the investment portfolio aims to beat the index in investing. Contrarily, passive investing promotes a passive strategy, such as purchasing an index fund designed to outperform the market continuously.

Both strategies have advantages and disadvantages, but only a few fund managers routinely outperform their benchmarks to make active management's higher costs worthwhile (Picardo, 2022).

Growth vs. value. High-growth businesses often have higher price-earnings (P/E) ratios than value businesses, which is why growth investors like to invest in them.

Value investors search for companies with P.E. ratios much lower than growth companies, and dividend yields are greater since these companies may be unpopular with short-term or long-term investors.

Risk appetite and risk tolerance. Every investment must take on a specific risk to fulfill its business objectives. Nonetheless, it is crucial to comprehend the distinction between risk tolerance and hunger. Boundaries are established by risk tolerance and appetite (Wire, 2022).

Risk tolerance focuses on acceptable risk fluctuations around particular objectives, whereas risk appetite takes a broad perspective on the overall level of risk deemed sufficient.

Think about the difference when you adhere to the posted speed limit on a highway. Even while traffic experts consider the speed limit to be safe and to meet the requirements of tolerable risk, or risk appetite, very few drivers do. Since they know this, most police officers show risk tolerance by allowing various speeds before issuing tickets to motorists.

Consider the risks you are ready to endure to accomplish your goals to establish your risk appetite. Every investor encounters some level of risk in their regular business operations, and knowing your risk tolerance helps you decide which risks to take and which to reduce.

An investor's level of risk tolerance is determined by how much volatility there is in the value of their investments. Risk tolerance is a crucial factor in investing since it frequently influences the kind and quantity of investments a person makes.

Whereas buying bonds, bond funds, and income funds is frequently associated with lesser risk tolerance, investing in equities, equity funds, and exchange-traded funds (ETFs) are commonly associated with higher risk tolerance.

Since all investments carry some level of risk, investors can better plan their entire portfolio and choose which investments to make by understanding their level of risk tolerance. Investors are categorized as aggressive, moderate, or conservative depending on how much risk they can accept (Twin, 2022).

Online risk assessment tools are available, including surveys or questionnaires dealing with risk. An investor may also look at historical returns for various asset classes to understand specific financial instruments' volatility.

The time horizon of an investor is one aspect that influences risk tolerance. Investors may see better returns when investing cautiously in higher-risk assets like equities and having a long time horizon for their financial goal. For short-term financial objectives, lower-risk cash investments might be appropriate.

The ability of an investor to generate money in the future and the presence of other assets like property, pension, Social Security, or a legacy impact risk tolerance. When an investor has access to additional, more reliable funding sources, they can invest some of their assets with higher risk.

Also, investors with a more extensive investment may be more risk-tolerant, since a larger portfolio has fewer potential losses than a smaller portfolio. As businesses cannot build one without the other, risk tolerance and risk appetite are inextricably linked.

Knowing what dangers your company faces through a thorough understanding of strategic risk assessment is essential for developing a strategy that will succeed or fail (Twin, 2022).

Consider your general desire for food while imagining your risk appetite. You know the foods you enjoy, how much your body can handle, and the best times to sate your appetite to prevent jitters.

You know what you can handle, what resources you need, and how you will get there. Risk appetite or the unique risks connected with a particular endeavor are more the focus of risk tolerance on a case-by-case basis.

Risk acceptance establishes the degree of danger you are willing to take with each specific risk, accepts the consequences or outcomes of that risk, should they materialize, and choose the tools and safeguards to lessen the impact of the risk. Your unique financial status determines how much financial risk you will take or your risk capacity (Twin, 2022).

Risk capacity is more adaptable and fluctuates depending on your financial and personal goals—and your schedule for reaching them—in contrast to risk tolerance, which may not alter throughout your life.

THINGS YOU SHOULD CONSIDER BEFORE INVESTING

Investments entail setting away your assets in equity, mutual funds, real estate, or commodities with the goal of capital appreciation (wealth growth) over a predetermined tenure determined by your personal preferences.

Given that someone else cannot describe your goals and select an appropriate solution, we have compiled essential guidelines to aid investment decision-making.

Personalize your financial roadmap. You must critically assess your financial situation in light of your obligations, priorities, way of life, and income.

Even though you must make some sacrifices to invest, it is never a good idea to push your spending past what is comfortable for you.

Determine the frequency and kind of investments based on a detailed analysis of your financial flow.

Discover your risk appetite. Each person's unique temperament and values define their capability to take risks. While many are risk-averse, certain people are more adept at taking risks.

A person's potential returns will be nearly guaranteed, and investing will be hassle-free if methods are laid up that match their level of risk tolerance. There is no point in putting your money in danger if it keeps you worrying about it at night (Reliance Smart Money, 2023).

Clarify your goals. This is an essential factor to consider before you make any investments.

Your objective may be short term, such as saving money for immediate requirements like a car purchase or a down payment on a home, or long-term, such as retirement planning or funding a child's education.

Whatever your goals are, clarifying your objectives makes them look simple or straightforward to accomplish.

Consider an appropriate mix of investments. Never put your entire portfolio at risk with a single investment strategy.

Whenever choosing mutual funds, consider the state of the market and divide your investment across different sectors or regions or put your money in a fund that does—this ensures prospective profits and assists in risk management.

Choose the investments you understand when mixing assets.

Conduct an individual-level evaluation. Even though we acknowledge the value of assessment and recommendations, remember that they cannot decide whether to invest (Reliance Smart Money, 2023).

Under no circumstances should you put your money in danger while relying on friends, fresh news, or professional guidance on television.

There is neither quick money nor a pre-made option. After thoroughly examining the individual level, you must base judgments on your needs.

Consider mutual fund investments. This is a good option for novice investors because they are expertly managed. They provide a variety of alluring qualities, such as diversification, which lowers risk while retaining potential profits.

Use SIP (Systematic Investment Planning) because it encourages discipline in investors and regularizes savings (Reliance Smart Money, 2023). Avoid derivatives, since they are not instruments for investing.

Stash some emergency capital and never borrow. Investing the entire sum in liquid assets over the long term is not a good idea because you must always be ready for any short-term cash necessity.

Never take out loans to finance investments. Recognize that by borrowing money, you significantly increase the risk involved with your financial arrangement.

Be cautious of scams and get-rich-quick schemes. Many phony investing choices are readily available today. Avoid being duped by promises that sound fancy. Be judicious in your decisions.

CREATING A DIVERSIFIED PORTFOLIO

By investing in many asset classes and various investments within those asset classes, diversification is a technique to minimize risk in your portfolio. A crucial component of any financial strategy, diversification finally acknowledges that no one can predict the future with certainty (Baker, 2022).

Investing in diversification wouldn't be needed if you could see into the future. The inevitable ups and downs of investing can be smoothed out, increasing the likelihood that you will adhere to your investment strategy and generate more significant returns.

Diversification of holdings reduces exposure to any one position and shields investors against significant fluctuations in essential industries. Trading both shares and bonds helps dealers diversify their portfolios. Adding options to a portfolio can be very advantageous during market turbulence (Baker, 2022).

Each trader's diversification approach should be appropriately matched to the demands of the portfolio because every investment portfolio is different. Because of the ample liquidity available through contract futures and options, any trading strategy may be customized to fit the long-term investment objectives of the trader.

Strategies for creating a balanced portfolio

Think beyond stocks vs. bonds. When most individuals think about a diverse investment portfolio, they probably picture a mix of stocks and bonds. While financial advisors have long used the proportion of stocks to bonds in a portfolio as a tool for risk management and diversification, consider diversification in more ways than just that.

Portfolios may, over time, become excessively exposed to specific asset classes or even to entire economic sectors and businesses. For example, because the underlying firm's investors held were linked to the same trends and forces in the late 1990s, their portfolios of diversified technology stocks needed to be genuinely diversified. Also, the Nasdaq Composite index, which primarily follows tech firms, declined almost 80% between its peak in March 2000 and its trough in the fall of 2002 (Baker, 2022).

Consider the industries and sectors to which your portfolio has exposure. To ensure correct diversity across your portfolio, consider scaling back any areas with excessive weighting.

Boost diversification using index funds. An inexpensive method to diversify your portfolio is through index funds. You can invest in a portfolio for nearly nothing by purchasing ETFs or mutual funds that follow extensive indexes like the S&P 500. This strategy is more straightforward than attempting to create a portfolio from the beginning and keeping track of the businesses and industries you are exposed to.

Index funds can also increase exposure to particular markets or industries where you may be underweight if you take a more active approach. These funds can be more costly than those that follow the most widely used indices. But if you want to manage your portfolio more actively, they can be a simple method to get exposure to specific industries.

Don't skip cash. Although frequently ignored, money has some advantages when developing a portfolio. Cash can offer safety in the case of a market selloff, although it will almost certainly lose value over time due to inflation.

Money could help your portfolio decrease less than the market averages during a downturn, depending on how much of it you have and any other investments you own.

Also, cash offers its owners flexibility. This shows that the value of having cash comes more from the alternatives it affords you when the environment is different in the future than it is from the current one.

Most people typically consider the available investment alternatives, omitting potential prospects. Yet, if you have some money in your portfolio, you can seize any investment discounts when the subsequent market slump occurs.

Improve your portfolio. Regularly increase your investment amounts. Employ dollar-cost averaging when investing. The peaks and troughs caused by market volatility are lessened with this strategy. This strategy aims to lower your investment risk by making the same amount of investments.

You put money into an individual portfolio of securities regularly when you use dollar-cost averaging. While using this method, you would purchase more shares at low prices and fewer at high prices (Palmer, 2023).

Think global. It is simple to overlook the rest of the globe when there are so many various investing choices accessible in the U.S. However, opportunities outside a nation's borders are becoming more alluring in a global economy. Investigating funds with an emphasis on developing markets in Europe or across the world can be worthwhile if your investment is solely oriented toward the United States.

Companies established may profit as nations like China expand more rapidly over the long term (Baker, 2022). It can also be a strategy to better safeguard yourself against unfavorable situations that only affect the United States. If the U.S. economy slows down, other markets might not be as negatively affected.

Naturally, the opposite is also accurate. Because of their immature financial systems and economies, emerging markets occasionally confront difficulties that can derail their long-term future growth. Nevertheless, diversifying your investment is about minimizing potential hiccups' impact.

Scan commissions. If trading is something other than your thing, be aware of what you're getting for your money. While some businesses charge transaction fees, others impose monthly costs, which can build up and seriously affect your revenue (Palmer, 2023).

Know what you are paying for and what you are getting in return. Keep in mind that only some options are the best. Be mindful of any adjustments to your fees, and stay informed.

Understand when to sell. Sound business practices include dollar-cost averaging and buying and holding. However, you should still consider the factors because your investments operate automatically (Palmer, 2023).

Keep up with your investments and be informed of changes in the general market environment. You must know what is occurring with the businesses you invest in. Also, by doing this, you will learn when to sell your investment, take your losses, and go on to your next one.

Ultimately, diversification is about embracing uncertainty and taking precautions to safeguard oneself. Assessing your investments a few times a year can help you focus and track your long-term plan and ensure your objectives are not dependent on just one or two investments.

As we've learned, becoming a millionaire is achievable through practical steps such as setting clear financial goals, getting advice when needed, using retirement accounts, and being intentional with your money. Don't just take our word for it. Let's look at real-life examples of average individuals who have become millionaires through hard work and thoughtful financial planning. These stories will inspire you to control your finances and reach your financial potential.

8

AVERAGE JOES AND JANES WHO BEAT THE JONESES AT THEIR OWN GAME

"You are the architect of your life."

— LAILAH GIFTY AKITA

Building wealth is more than knowing the process of becoming a millionaire. What matters most is executing your plans via saving and investing—this helps compound your money.

Cultivating a habit of saving and investing is the first step to becoming a millionaire, which can significantly affect your path. This chapter showcases real-life examples of average individuals who have become millionaires through hard work, disciplined saving, smart spending, and strategic investing, inspiring and motivating you toward financial success.

RONALD READ

Read was a janitor and attendant at a local Vermont gas depot. He built an $8 million fortune by investing in popular brands.

With his passing, he left a sizable portion of his riches to a local clinic and library, shocking a neighborhood unaware of his wealth.

Locals regarded Ronald Read as a taciturn individual who enjoyed driving his used Toyota Yaris about the Vermont hamlet of Brattleboro and chopping wood. The townspeople didn't perceive him as the kind of man with considerable cash to spend.

Most Brattleboro neighbors were surprised to discover that the 92-year-estate donated $4.8 million to the community clinic and another $1.2 million to the Brooks Memorial Library when Read died in June 2014.

The executor of Read's property, Laurie Rowell, stated that she understood why each community member was shocked by the information. You wouldn't realize he was wealthy from the way he looked. He used to fasten his fleece jackets with safety pins.

Read claimed to have money at first, but nobody believed him because of how he appeared—a well-used coat, a plaid shirt, and a cowboy hat. Read was well known for being thrifty. Philip Brown, one of Read's step kids, claimed not to have known how well-off his dad was.

Never make assumptions about people at the other end of the table based on appearance.

Read only made investments in things he understood would yield a profit. So how did Read end up with a million dollars?

His meager savings had grown to nearly $8 million before he died not because he was an expert stock picker. He became rich over time by taking advantage of compound interest and being a buy and hold investor.

GRACE GRONER

Grace grew up among her neighbors since she was an orphan. She was 25 when she took a secretary role with Abbott Pharmaceuticals, a position she held for 43 years.

Since Abbot sold shares, Grace Groner purchased $180 worth of her employer's stock. The money afforded three shares. She was in her first year in the firm when she bought the shares.

Grace Groner managed to save $180 despite working as a secretary. She purchased the shares with cash and reinvested the dividends.

Since she purchased interest-generating stocks, she made a particular profit percentage annually. After receiving those payments, she used them to acquire more shares—she repeated this every year.

She continued reinvesting her dividends for 75 years before she died and made over $7 million.

Grace Groner, an Abbott Labs secretary, amassed a $7 million fortune in this way and became a millionaire. Her secret to success was reinvesting every dividend income so that it could grow over time.

ANNE SCHEIBER

Anne performed auditing duties for the IRS. In 1944, when she was 51 years old, she retired and spent the following 50 years concentrating on maintaining her investments.

She passed away, aged 101, leaving behind a dividend investment portfolio valued at over $22 million. At the period of her passing, the investment was producing over $750,000 in cash dividends annually.

Among all-time's greatest return investors, Anne Scheiber has had great success. After her father passed away due to financial losses on property investments, her mom raised Anne. She began her job as a clerk at the tender age of 15 and joined the IRS.

Families of that period gave their boys' further education a priority. So, Anne Scheiber had to endure and pay for her own tuition.

She invested in herself in finishing night school and subsequently passing the bar. She understood that because she was a Jewish woman, she would only develop professionally a little, notwithstanding her good job efficiency and excellent qualifications.

Anne spent 19 years working for the IRS but had yet to receive a promotion or salary worth over $3,150 annually because of the bias that existed then. Because of her tough upbringing and constant need to support herself, she probably concluded that investing was the best way to make a name for herself.

Long before she passed away, she knew she would donate her nest egg to a good cause. She would remark that someday, after she'd been long gone, some ladies would no longer struggle to provide for themselves.

Anne maintained a top rate of savings, thus ensuring that she gathered the first funds needed to build her nest egg. She impressively saved somewhere about 80% of her income.

She held holdings in over 100 companies and recognizable brands like Coca-Cola, PepsiCo, and Bristol-Myers. She invested in business sectors she was familiar with, like pharmaceuticals, beverages, and entertainment.

Anne concentrated on businesses with renowned brands that increase profits. As a result, the company could raise its intrinsic value and pay out higher dividends. Her plan involved regular stock purchases that she held onto for years. She can fully leverage compounding, thanks to this. Her dividend reinvestment further compounded her capital and income.

In the 1980s, she began putting her considerable dividend income into municipal bonds, which offered a yearly interest rate of 8% that was tax free. Her $750,000 in annual investment income combined with earnings and dividends.

Anne drastically reduced spending because she didn't receive raises or promotions. She saw the straightforward math underlying early retirement. She wore vintage clothing, saved money on food, and spent 51 years in her rent-controlled apartment after retirement. Her hobbies were reading, investigating businesses, watching movies, and studying stock reports.

CURT DEGERMAN

Curt appeared to be a lowly tin collector to the outside world. The elderly Swede spent 30 years collecting bottles and tin cans for money in the neighborhoods of Skelleftea in northern Sweden while wearing a blue jacket and worn-out slacks.

Most people thought of him as being just another common street beggar. Yet, he left his relative over $1.4 million when he passed away. How did this happen through thrift and intelligent investing?

Mr. Degerman spent considerable time in the neighborhood library reading business publications and researching the stock market in between collecting cans. He understood stock.

Curt Degerman used recycling profits to buy mutual funds. He also purchased 124 gold bars and accumulated his money in a savings account. He had a bicycle and no mortgage, which made saving money simpler.

That is the traditional fairy tale of frugality and cunning.

A heart attack claimed Mr. Degerman's life in 2008. In his will, he transferred his entire estate to a relative who frequently visited him in his later years.

Curt Degerman never finished college or got married. He led a modest life, riding his bike everywhere. His tale illustrates how being frugal and exercising wise money management may result in wealth accumulation.

MORAL OF THE STORY

If you study these self-made millionaires, you see they share these common themes.

Frugal lifestyle. These people lived a simple and thrifty lifestyle, avoiding excessive spending and saving as much as possible. A thrifty person will be more aware of the advantages of the items or services gained than the expenses paid. A modest way of life will hasten your progress toward financial freedom.

You learn to make thoughtful financial judgments through frugal living. The result is that a thrifty person will set away more money for savings or investments.

Living simply and following the principle of modest living is preferable to living for the sake of status. If you need more certainty about using a credit card to make a purchase, you don't have to buy expensive clothing. Future tension and financial strain will only come from maintaining a lifestyle outside your means.

Investing. All the self-made millionaires invested their money in various forms, including stocks, mutual funds, and gold bars. Investing is a successful approach to using your cash and increasing your fortune. Your funds may grow in worth and beat inflation if you make wise investment decisions.

Compounding's effectiveness and the risk-return exchange are the leading causes of investing's higher growth prospects. When income or profits are generated by an asset and then reinvested, compounding takes place. Once received, these profits or returns produce additional yields. So, compounding helps investments build an income from prior income. For example, if you reinvest gains from a stock you purchased that pays dividends, you may benefit from the compounding effect.

Compounding. The self-made millionaires above reinvested their earnings and allowed their investments to compound over time, accumulating significant wealth. Although keeping some extra cash may be enticing, reinvesting your income can be beneficial over the long term.

The force of compounding allows dividend reinvestment to boost long-term gains significantly. Your earnings enable you to purchase additional shares, and this cycle repeats itself as you raise your income and buy more shares.

Patience. They were patient and disciplined in their wealth-building approach, avoiding impulsive decisions and sticking to their long-term goals.

People use many financial jargons that aid in choosing the finest stock or mutual fund when discussing investments. These financial measurements can be helpful, but we must also remember to exercise patience, a crucial quality.

Patience is essential for a profitable investment in the long run. Making investing decisions with patience entails putting off the impulse to act immediately. Good investors typically take their time to observe, evaluate markets and patterns over time, and make decisions. By exercising patience, investors can prosper more and maintain their financial security.

Reinvesting dividends. All the self-made millionaires reinvested their dividends, allowing their wealth to grow even further.

Smart financial planning. All the personalities discussed above made wise financial decisions, such as avoiding debt and living a mortgage-free life.

People can analyze possibilities and make wise decisions for their economic circumstances with healthy cash awareness and choice abilities.

A focus on understanding. If you carefully consider the self-made millionaires above, you will notice that they invested in companies and industries they understood, avoiding high-risk investments.

These average millionaires did not engage in lifestyle inflation or try to chase the Joneses. They lived frugal lifestyles and made wise financial decisions.

So, now that you've seen the incredible stories of everyday people who've become millionaires, it's time to take what you've learned and put it into action. It's time to turn inspiration into motivation and build the financial future you've always dreamed of. You will likely be amazed at the peace you feel by not always chasing the next purchase. The longer you apply lessons in these stories the easier it is to save for the future and love what you have. Over time, you will grow your net worth to be able to easily keep up with the Joneses and not even feel the urge to.

CONCLUSION

Let the Joneses Think They are Winning teaches an average person how to become a millionaire and live the life they have always dreamed of by simply leveraging the power of time.

The book addresses the root cause of financial issues—the societal pressure to keep up with consumer culture. By tackling this issue head-on and encouraging people to examine their spending habits and beliefs, this book empowers individuals to break free from the cycle of consumerism and truly achieve financial success.

The key takeaways of the book include:

- Practical tips to enhance your money management skills, set clear, achievable financial goals, and accomplish them.
- Innovative strategies to stay inspired and motivated to regulate your finances and reach your financial goals.
- Clever ways to debunk common myths about wealth creation and discover a clearer picture of what it takes to become a millionaire.
- Actionable and straightforward steps to building wealth and achieving financial stability.
- Creative procedures for breaking free from consumer culture, overcoming the *Joneses mentality*, and focusing on healthy financial goals without comparing yourself to others.

You see the people in the previous chapter—they're just like you and me. They went to work every day, lived modestly, and saved their money. And yet, they all became millionaires. They didn't have trust funds, they didn't marry into money, and they certainly weren't trying to chase the Joneses. They understood the power of saving, investing, and avoiding lifestyle inflation. And look at where it got them.

As for me (Guy Edwards) and my wife, we are on track to retire before 50, with a net worth of over $4 million. And we're just a couple of ordinary people!

These real-life stories prove anyone can become a millionaire if they stay out of consumer culture, save early and often, and make small changes in their spending habits. You don't have to be the showiest person in the room to be the richest. It just takes discipline and intention.

If you feel inadequate, are not measuring up to societal expectations and cultural norms, or face social pressure and constantly sense the urge to chase the Joneses, I hope this book provided the remedies you craved.

Take control of your finances immediately. You have the power within you to become a millionaire, just like all those other average folks who have done it before you.

The tools required to improve your life lie in your hands—use them! Apply the tips and strategies in this book to bid consumer culture goodbye and embrace financial independence. If you can save like they won't now, you can live like they can't in retirement.

Kindly hit us with a review on Amazon if you enjoy this book.

REFERENCES

Appleby, D. (2023, January 15). *Roth IRA vs. Traditional IRA: Key Differences.* Retrieved March 1, 2023, from https://www.investopedia.com/retirement/roth-vs-traditional-ira-which-is-right-for-you/

Ashford, K. (2022, July 14). *The Life-Changing Magic Of Compound Interest.* Retrieved February 22, 2023, from https://www.forbes.com/advisor/investing/compound-interest/

Awanis, S., Schlegelmilch, B., & Cui, C. (2018, January 23). *There's no shame in being materialistic – it could benefit society.* Retrieved February 21, 2023, from https://www.google.com/amp/s/theconversation.com/amp/theres-no-shame-in-being-materialistic-it-could-benefit-society-89996

Baker, B. (2022, July 26). *6 tips for diversifying your investment portfolio.* Retrieved March 4, 2023, from https://www.bankrate.com/investing/tips-for-diversifying-your-portfolio/

Becker, J. (n.d.). *9 Intentional Ways to Challenge Consumerism in Your Life.* Retrieved February 24, 2023, from https://www.becomingminimalist.com/less-consumerism/

Bell, A. (2022, April 7). *6 Reasons Why You Need a Budget.* Retrieved February 23, 2023, from https://www.investopedia.com/financial-edge/1109/6-reasons-why-you-need-a-budget.aspx

Be the Budget. (n.d.). *10 Best Benefits Of Frugal Living.* Retrieved February 21, 2023, from https://bethebudget.com/frugal-living-benefits/

Caesar, T. (2019, April 29). *8 Reasons to Make a Shopping List.* Retrieved February 23, 2023, from https://www.positivelendingsolutions.com.au/resources/information-centre/8-reasons-to-make-a-shopping-list/

Canada Life (n.d.). *What are the benefits of saving money early?* Retrieved February 22, 2023, from https://www.canadalife.com/blog/investing-saving/benefits-saving-money-early.html

Carlson, S. (2022, October 25). *How Delaying Gratification Can Help You Achieve Your Money Goals.* Retrieved February 24, 2023, from https://fulcrumfinancialgroup.com/blog/how-delaying-gratification

Carter, S. (2018, March 15). *Social media may be making you overspend—and it's not just because of the ads.* Retrieved February 21, 2023, from https://www.cnbc.com/2018/03/15/social-media-may-make-you-overspend-and-its-not-just-because-of-ads.html

Chen, J. (2023, February 24). *What Is a Brokerage Account? Definition, How to Choose, and Types.* Retrieved March 1, 2023, from https://www.investopedia.com/terms/b/brokerageaccount.asp

Choice Wealth. (n.d.). *High Net-Worth Individuals: Are You Missing Opportunities in Your Financial Planning?* Retrieved February 27, 2023, from https://bankwithchoice.com/wealth-blog/high-net-worth-individuals-are-you-missing-opportunities-in-your-financial-planning/

Cook, J. & Grimsley, S. (2021, December 23). *What is the consumer culture theory?* Retrieved February 21, 2023, from https://study.com/learn/lesson/consumer-culture-overview-theory.html#:~:text=What%20is%20an%20example%20of,and%20how%20much%20they%20have

Cote, C. (2022, June 16). *Time Value of Money (TVM): A Primer.* Retrieved February 22, 2023, from https://online.hbs.edu/blog/post/time-value-of-money

CreditNinja. (2022, July 23). *What Are the Negative Effects of Impulse Buying?* Retrieved February 23, 2023, from https://www.creditninja.com/what-are-the-negative-effects-of-impulse-buying/

Cruze, R. (2022, June 27). *Impulse Buying: Why We Do It and How to Stop.* Retrieved February 23, 2023, from https://www.ramseysolutions.com/budgeting/stop-impulse-buys

Cruze, R. (2022, July 18). *Shopping Addiction: Symptoms, Causes and How to Address It.* Retrieved February 21, 2023, from https://www.ramseysolutions.com/budgeting/shopping-addiction

Cruze, R. (2022, December, 22). *How to Set Financial Goals.* Retrieved March 1, 2023, from https://www.ramseysolutions.com/personal-growth/setting-financial-goals

Cueto, C. (2022, December 30). *9 Steps to Developing a Positive Money Mindset.* Retrieved February 27, 2023, from https://www.prosper.com/blog/better-money-habits-positive-money-mindset

DeAngelis, T. (2004, June 5). *Consumerism and its discontents.* Retrieved February 21, 2023, from https://www.apa.org/monitor/jun04/discontents

Farrington, R. (2023, January 30). *5 Benefits of Investing.* Retrieved March 4, 2023, from https://thecollegeinvestor.com/16912/5-benefits-of-investing/

Feeling Financial. (n.d.). *Types of Investments.* Retrieved March 4, 2023, from https://feelingfinancial.com/types-of-investments/

Fernando, J. (2022, July 19). *The Power of Compound Interest: Calculations and Examples.* Retrieved February 22, 2023, from https://www.investopedia.com/terms/c/compoundinterest.asp

Fernando, J. (2022, September 28). *Time Value of Money Explained with Formula and Examples.* Retrieved February 22, 2023, from https://www.investopedia.com/terms/t/timevalueofmoney.asp

Finance Over Fifty. (n.d.). *How Do Limiting Beliefs Harm Us? Here Are 5 Ways.* Retrieved February 27, 2023, from https://financeoverfifty.com/the-high-cost-of-limiting-beliefs/

Franklin Templeton. (n.d.). *What is the Importance of Retirement Planning?* Retrieved March 1, 2023, from https://www.franklintempletonindia.com/investor-education/planning-for-retirement/article/headstart-15/what-is-the-importance-of-retirement-planning

Frugal Woods. (2015, September 8). *11 Benefits of Frugality That Have Nothing To Do With Money.* Retrieved February 21, 2023, from https://www.frugalwoods.com/2015/09/08/11-benefits-of-frugality-that-have-nothing-to-do-with-money/

FSCB (2021, September 24). *What Does It Mean to Achieve Financial Freedom?* Retrieved February 21, 2023, from https://www.fscb.com/blog/what-does-it-look-like-to-achieve-financial-freedom

Halimi, E. (2022, August 9). *Can Compound Interest Really Make Me a Millionaire?* Retrieved March 1, 2023, from https://www.alinea-invest.com/blog/can-compound-interest-really-make-me-a-millionaire

Hayes, A. (2022, September 30). *Investment Basics Explained With Types to Invest in.* Retrieved March 4, 2023, from https://www.investopedia.com/terms/i/investment.asp

Heyford, S. (2022, May 23). *Understanding the Time Value of Money.* Retrieved February 22, 2023, from https://www.investopedia.com/articles/03/082703.asp

Higgs, K. (2021, January 11). *A brief history of consumer culture.* Retrieved February 21, 2023, from https://thereader.mitpress.mit.edu/a-brief-history-of-consumer-culture/

Holik, M. (2021, December 16). *The Urge to Splurge: 8 Ways to Resist Your Budget Killers.* Retrieved February 23, 2023, from https://stateecu.com/the-urge-to-splurge-how-to-resist/

Home Business. (2019, February 8). *10 Important Benefits of Saving Money.* Retrieved February 21, 2023, from https://homebusinessmag.com/money/personal-finance/10-important-benefits-saving-money/

Houston, M. (2021, October 28). *How Your Financial Values Need To Tie Into Your Life.* Retrieved February 21, 2023, from https://www.forbes.com/sites/melissahouston/2021/10/28/how-your-financial-values-need-to-tie-into-your-life/?sh=2fea831db418

IGI Global. (n.d.). *What is consumer culture?* Retrieved February 21, 2023, from https://www.igi-global.com/dictionary/consumer-culture/43954

Kagan, J. (2021, November 26). *SIMPLE IRA: Definition, How Small Businesses Use, and Drawbacks.* Retrieved March 1, 2023, from https://www.investopedia.com/terms/s/simple-ira.asp

Kenton, W. (2020, July 19). *Lifestyle Inflation*. Retrieved February 24, 2023, from https://www.investopedia.com/terms/l/lifestyle-inflation.asp

Kilroy, A. (2022, July 14). *Tips for Overcoming Bad Financial Decisions*. Retrieved February 27, 2023, from https://www.sofi.com/learn/content/overcoming-these-15-horrible-financial-decisions/

Lake, R. (2022, October 19). *Budgets: Everything You Need To Know*. Retrieved February 23, 2023, from https://www.thebalancemoney.com/how-to-make-a-budget-1289587

Machina, Z. (n.d.). *Why It's Important to Surround Yourself with the Right People*. Retrieved February 24, 2023, from https://phase.undock.com/why-its-important-to-surround-yourself-with-the-right-people/

Madan, S. (2017, July 23). *The psychology behind the urge to splurge*. Retrieved February 24, 2023, from https://www.livemint.com/Sundayapp/BHJO2lUEWyP0haqJf8FruN/The-urge-to-splurge.html

Mawer, R. (2022, September 12). *3 myths holding people back from becoming millionaires*. Retrieved February 25, 2023, from https://www.fastcompany.com/90822382/3-myths-holding-people-back-from-becoming-millionaires

Maximize Minimalism (n.d.). *7 reasons why people become obsessed with material possessions*. Retrieved February 21, 2023, from https://maximizeminimalism.com/7-reasons-why-people-are-obsessed-material-possessions/

Mercadante, K. (2023, January 9). *7 Most Popular Employer-Sponsored Retirement Plans*. Retrieved March 1, 2023, from https://investorjunkie.com/retirement/employer-sponsored-retirement-plans/#:~:text=401(k)%20Plan,least%20a%20partial%20employer%20match

My Money Yard. (2022, October 23). *Is Lifestyle Inflation Always Bad?* Retrieved February 24, 2023, from https://mymoneyyard.com/lifestyle-inflation/

O'Shea, A. (2023, January 5). *What Is a Simplified Employee Pension Plan? How SEP IRAs Work*. Retrieved March 1, 2023, from https://www.nerdwallet.com/article/investing/what-is-a-sep-ira

O'Shea, B. & Schwahn, L. (2022, December 2). *Budgeting 101: How to Budget Money*. Retrieved February 23, 2023, from https://www.nerdwallet.com/article/finance/how-to-budget

Palmer, B. (2022, December 18). *6 Steps to Become a Millionaire by 30*. Retrieved March 1, 2023, from https://www.investopedia.com/financial-advisor/how-much-save-to-become-millionaire/

Palmer, B. (2023, February 26). *5 Tips for Diversifying Your Portfolio*. Retrieved March 4, 2023, from https://www.investopedia.com/articles/03/072303.asp

Paul, T. (2022, September 12). *Here's why it's so important to start saving and investing in your 20s*. Retrieved February 22, 2023, from https://www.cnbc.com/select/why-you-should-start-saving-in-your-20s/

Picardo, E. (2022, July 22). *Investing Explained: Types of Investments and How To Get Started*. Retrieved March 4, 2023, from https://www.investopedia.com/terms/i/investing.asp

Positively Frugal. (2022, December 6). *8 Benefits of Being Debt Free*. Retrieved February 21, 2023, from https://positivelyfrugal.com/benefits-of-being-debt-free/

Ramsey Solutions. (2022, February 23). *Millionaire Myth Busters*. Retrieved February 25, 2023, from https://www.ramseysolutions.com/retirement/millionaire-myth-busters

Ramsey Solutions. (2022, May 6). *The National Study of Millionaires*. Retrieved February 25, 2023, from https://www.ramseysolutions.com/retirement/the-national-study-of-millionaires-research

Ramsey Solutions. (2022, June 27). *Does Couponing Really Save You Money?* Retrieved February 23, 2023, from https://www.ramseysolutions.com/budgeting/is-couponing-worth-your-time

Ramsey Solutions. (2022, July 22). *Lifestyle Inflation: More Money, Same Problems*. Retrieved February 24, 2023, from https://www.ramseysolutions.com/budgeting/lifestyle-inflation

Ramsey Solutions. (2023, January 10). *How to Save Money: 23 Simple Tips*. Retrieved February 23, 2023, from https://www.ramseysolutions.com/budgeting/the-secret-to-saving-money

Ramsey Solutions. (2023, January 10). *Ways to Save on Home Expenses.* Retrieved February 23, 2023, from https://www.ramseysolutions.com/budgeting/save-on-home-expenses

Ramsey Solutions. (2023, February 3). *How to Make a Budget: Your Step-by-Step Guide.* Retrieved February 23, 2023, from https://www.ramseysolutions.com/budgeting/how-to-make-a-budget

Reliance Smart Money. (2023, March 3). *Ten Things to Consider Before You Make Decisions of Investing Money.* Retrieved March 4, 2023, from https://www.reliancesmartmoney.com/Insights/blog/rsm-articles/2020/01/29/ten-things-to-consider-before-you-make-investing-decisions

Richmond, S. (2022, December 1). *Why Save for Retirement in Your 20s?* Retrieved March 1, 2023, from https://www.investopedia.com/articles/personal-finance/040315/why-save-retirement-your-20s.asp

Roomer, J. (n.d.). *6 Common Myths About Becoming A Millionaire Keeping You From Building Wealth.* Retrieved February 27, 2023, from https://medium.com/wealthwise/6-common-myths-about-becoming-a-millionaire-keeping-you-from-building-wealth-decfd42166ca

Rose, J. (2019, May 10). *5 Millionaire Myths Keeping You Poor.* Retrieved February 25, 2023, from https://www.forbes.com/sites/jrose/2019/05/10/5-millionaire-myths-keeping-you-poor/?sh=2ae8577e2bf5

Schwahn, L. (2022, December 2). *Average Net Worth by Age: How Do You Compare?* Retrieved March 15, 2023, from https://www.nerdwallet.com/article/finance/average-net-worth-by-age

Sharma, A. (2022, October 10). *Effects of Advertising on Consumer Behavior.* Retrieved February 21, 2023, from https://www.linkedin.com/pulse/effects-advertising-consumer-behavior-aman-sharma/

Shelton, B. (n.d.). *Celebrate Small Wins to Track Progress on Long-Term Goals.* Retrieved February 24, 2023, from https://www.buxtonco.com/blog/celebrate-small-wins-to-track-progress-on-long-term-goals

Shukla, A. (2022, June 11). *The effects of consumerism.* Retrieved February 21, 2023, from https://www.paggu.com/business/world-economy/the-effects-of-consumerism/

Srinivasan, H. (2022, August 23). *How to Stop Impulse Buying.* Retrieved February 23, 2023, from https://www.realsimple.com/work-life/money/saving/how-to-stop-impulse-buying

Surbhi, S. (2017, October 21). *Difference Between Needs and Wants.* Retrieved February 24, 2023, from https://keydifferences.com/difference-between-needs-and-wants.html

Tardy, J. (2016, December 3). *Become a millionaire by busting these 5 myths.* Retrieved February 25, 2023, from https://www.marketwatch.com/story/become-a-millionaire-by-busting-these-5-myths-2016-11-29

Thrivent. (2022, April 27). *What is lifestyle inflation & how does it affect your budget?* Retrieved February 24, 2023, from https://www.thrivent.com/insights/budgeting-saving/what-is-lifestyle-inflation-and-how-does-it-affect-your-budget

Thrivent. (2022, July 8). *The differences between real estate, stocks, bonds & mutual funds.* Retrieved March 4, 2023, from https://www.thrivent.com/insights/investing/the-differences-between-real-estate-stocks-bonds-and-mutual-funds

Torabi, F. (2011, June 10). *Needs vs. Wants? Explaining the Urge to Splurge.* Retrieved February 24, 2023, from https://www.cbsnews.com/news/needs-vs-wants-explaining-the-urge-to-splurge/

Twin, A. (2022, July 7). *What Is Risk Tolerance, and Why Does It Matter?* Retrieved March 4, 2023, from https://www.investopedia.com/terms/r/risktolerance.asp

UFCU. (2020, May 28). *Celebrating small financial wins.* Retrieved February 24, 2023, from https://utahfirst.com/celebrating-small-financial-wins/

Wells Fargo. (n.d.). *Why Invest.* Retrieved March 4, 2023, from https://www.wellsfargo.com/goals-investing/why-invest/#:~:text=Why%20investing%20matters,and%20the%20risk%2Dreturn%20tradeoff

Wemyss, S. (2022, May 4). *Patience & Discipline: Two Vital Traits of Every Successful Investor.* Retrieved February 24, 2023, from https://www.prosolution.com.au/patience-discipline/

Westpac (2021, October 5). *The benefits of being debt-free.* Retrieved February 21, 2023, from https://www.westpac.com.au/help/lifemoments/recovery/respond/benefits-of-being-debt-free/

Wire, A. (2022, August 8). *Risk tolerance vs risk appetite: The difference explained.* Retrieved March 4, 2023, from https://www.irmagazine.com/reporting/risk-tolerance-vs-risk-appetite-difference-explained

Yeager, J. (n.d.). *12 Ways to Avoid Impulse Buying.* Retrieved February 23, 2023, from https://www.aarp.org/money/budgeting-saving/info-10-2010/savings_challenge_tips_for_impulse_shopping.html

Made in the USA
Middletown, DE
28 October 2024